SMART-OPEDIA Junior

THE AMAZING BOOK ABOUT EVERYTHING

MAPLE
TREE
PRESS

Maple Tree Press books are published by Owlkids Books Inc.
10 Lower Spadina Ave., Suite 400, Toronto, Ontario M5V 2Z2
www.mapletreepress.com

Maple Tree Press Edition © 2008
Original edition: *Ma petite encyclopédie Dokeo 3–6 ans*
© 2006 by Éditions Nathan, Paris, France

Distributed in Canada by Raincoast Books
9050 Shaughnessy Street, Vancouver, British Columbia V6P 6E5

Distributed in the United States by Publishers Group West
1700 Fourth Street, Berkeley, California 94710

Cataloguing in Publication Data
Smart-opedia junior

Includes index.
Translation of: Dokéo, 3-6 ans.

ISBN 978-1-897349-30-4

1. Children's encyclopedias and dictionaries. 2. Encyclopedias and dictionaries.

AG6.S623 2008   j031   C2008-902045-6

Library of Congress Control Number: 2008925718

Text for North American Edition: The editors of Maple Tree Press

Cover design: Claudia Dávila

Illustrators:
Our Bodies (page 6–29) and A House to Live In (page 30–45): **Virginie Guérin**
In the City (page 46–65): **Catherine Chardonnay**
In the City (page 66–79): **Élodie Durand**
History (page 80–99) and The Universe (page 170–181): **Rémi Saillard**
A World of Plants and Animals (100–133): **Nathalie Choux**
A Big, Wide World (page 134–169): **Didier Balicevic**

We acknowledge the financial support of the Canada Council for the
Arts, the Ontario Arts Council, the Government of Canada through the
Book Publishing Industry Development Program (BPIDP), and the
 ONTARIO ARTS COUNCIL
CONSEIL DES ARTS DE L'ONTARIO
Government of Ontario through the Ontario Media Development Corporation's Book Initiative for our publishing activities.

Printed in China

A   B   C   D   E   F

Introduction

Soon you will be learning amazing things about the world around you.
Watch for these fun features throughout this book:

Figure It Out!

Have fun with puzzles and games. Spot hidden animals, read Egyptian hieroglyphics, make movie sound effects!

What About You?

You are a very special person. What are your favorite colors? What's your birthday? What was the first word you said?

Did You Know?

Eye-opening facts about animals, plants, people, and places add more information — to make you even smarter.

Number Time!

Discover the size of a lion, how many blocks in a pyramid, and the speed of your sneeze!

Kids' Question

Why does the Moon change shape? How do fish breathe underwater? Why are leaves green?

Find answers to real questions like these, asked by kids just like you.

Contents

Kids' Questions

Our Bodies

What a crowd on the beach! There are grandparents, there are babies, kids and their families, little people and big people, all kinds of people.... Each one is different from everyone else. But everyone has a body that works the same way yours does.

Figure It Out!

Holly has brown hair. She is five years old.

She is putting a flag on her sand castle.

Her cousin Simon is a redhead.

Stretched out on his towel, he is eating an ice-cream.

Holly's mother has long, blonde hair.

She is reading a book.

Holly's father has curly, brown hair.

He is windsurfing.

Holly's Front

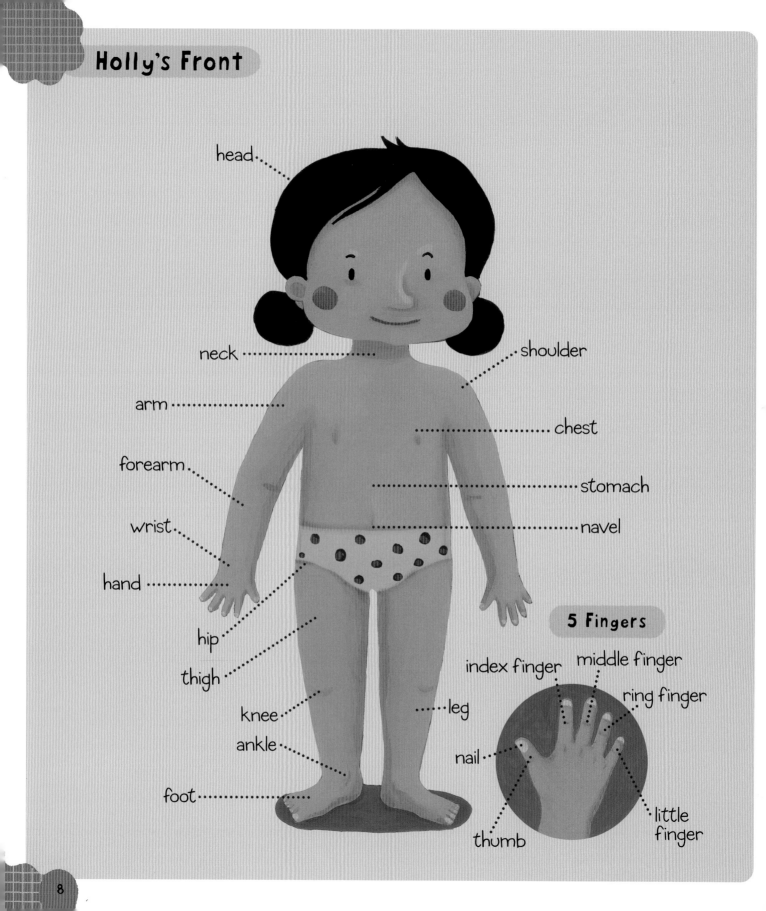

head

neck

arm

forearm

wrist

hand

hip

thigh

knee

ankle

foot

shoulder

chest

stomach

navel

leg

nail

thumb

5 Fingers

index finger

middle finger

ring finger

little finger

Simon's Front

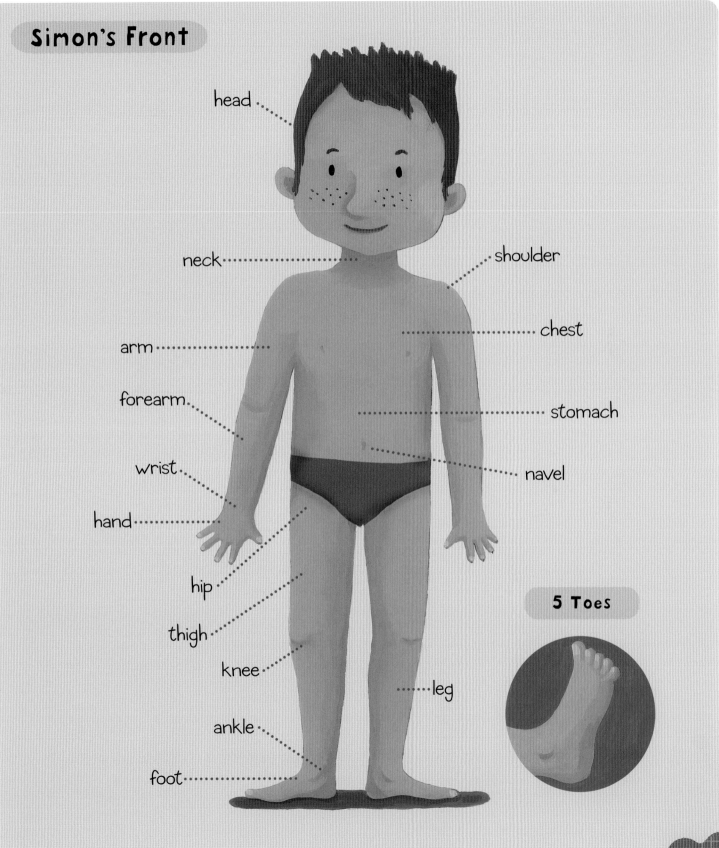

head

neck

shoulder

arm

chest

forearm

stomach

wrist

navel

hand

hip

thigh

knee

leg

ankle

foot

5 Toes

9

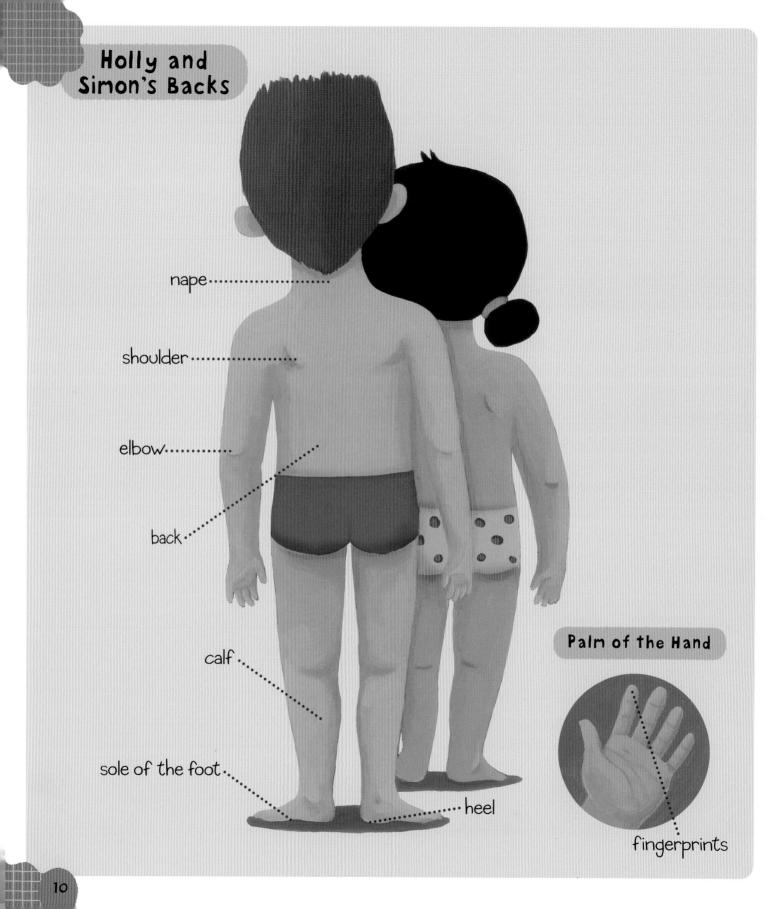

Holly and Simon's Backs

nape

shoulder

elbow

back

calf

sole of the foot

heel

Palm of the Hand

fingerprints

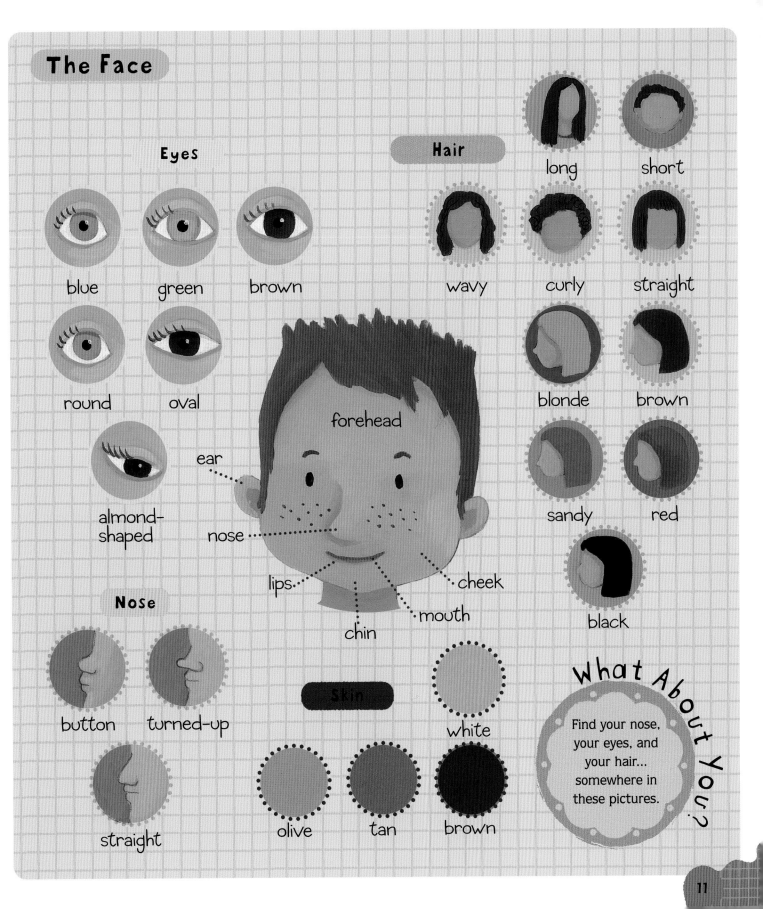

The Face

Eyes

blue   green   brown

round   oval

almond-shaped

Hair

long   short

wavy   curly   straight

blonde   brown

sandy   red

black

forehead

ear

nose

lips

chin

mouth

cheek

Nose

button   turned-up

straight

Skin

white

olive   tan   brown

What About You?
Find your nose, your eyes, and your hair... somewhere in these pictures.

11

Nine Months Till Baby Is Born

Marie and Jason love each other. They love their daughter Holly very much. "Being a family is great!" they say happily.

Number Time!

A woman is pregnant with a baby for 9 months (270 days).

For animals, it's different:

Hamster: 15 days

Dog: 63 days

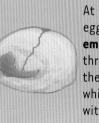
Dolphin: 365 days

Elephant: 620 days

1 Good News!

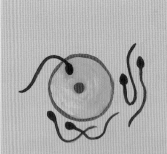

Marie feels tired. A blood test shows that she is going to have a baby.

One of Jason's **sperm** has joined with an **egg** in Marie's womb. The tiny egg will become a baby.

2 Eating for Two

Marie and Jason go out to eat with their friend. Marie does not drink wine, and eats lots of healthy food.

At 1 month old, the egg has become an **embryo**. It gets food through a tube called the **umbilical cord**, which connects it with its mother.

3 Funny Pictures

Marie goes to have her first **ultrasound**, a medical exam where she sees the baby on a screen.

By the time it is 3 months old, the embryo has become a **fetus**. With a head, arms, and legs, the fetus already looks like a little person.

4 Oh—Baby Kicked Me!

Today Marie felt the baby move for the first time. What a surprise!

At 4 months old, the baby can wave arms and legs around in the **amniotic fluid**. There's still lots of room.

5 Boy or Girl?

At the second **ultrasound**, Jason and Marie find out they are expecting…a boy!

Now 5 months old, the baby sucks his thumb and recognizes different tastes in the amniotic fluid.

6 Hello in There?

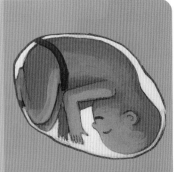

Jason sings a song to the baby. Holly wants to tell her brother a story, even though it is her bedtime!

At 7 months old the baby's eyes are open and he can hear all kinds of sounds.

7 He's Coming…

Marie stops working. Her stomach has grown very big. She is getting ready to have the baby.

During the last months the baby grows a lot. At 9 months old, he is ready to come out!

8 He's Here!

When Marie begins to feel that the baby is coming, Jason takes her to the hospital for the **birth**. A few hours later, they hold their son for the first time.

Kids' Question

What are twins?

Sometimes one of the mother's eggs divides in two and grows into two embryos. When the babies are born they look exactly alike. These are **identical twins**.

Other times two eggs develop in the mother's womb, and two babies are born at the same time. But these babies don't look exactly like each other. They are **fraternal twins**.

Baby Joins the Family

Ethan is the name that Marie and Jason choose for their new baby boy. Now the family is growing!

Marie, Jason, and Holly Todd are thrilled to announce the arrival of their son and Holly's little brother, Ethan.

Born on June 5 at 6 p.m. Please join us in welcoming Ethan to the world.

What About You?

What date and time were you born?

Tell Everyone!

Marie and Jason announce Ethan's birth to all their family and friends.

Jason sends pictures of the new baby to everyone by email.

Jason also registers the birth of his son with the government.

Everyone Wants to See Him

In Marie's hospital room, the whole family crowds around to see the new baby. Holly sulks a little. She is happy to have a baby brother, but no one is paying any attention to her!

Family Tree

Meet everyone in Holly and Ethan's family on their family tree.

Grandma Katie and Grandpa David
These are Marie's parents, and Holly and Ethan's **maternal grandparents.**

Grandpa Peter and Grandma Anne
These are Jason's parents and Holly and Ethan's **paternal grandparents.**

William and Susie
Susie is Marie's sister, and Holly and Ethan's **aunt.** William is her husband, and their **uncle.**

Marie and Jason
These are Holly and Ethan's **parents.**

Simon and Emma
Simon and Emma are William and Susie's children, and Holly and Ethan's **cousins.**

Holly and Ethan
Holly and Ethan are **sister** and **brother.**

Figure It Out!
Use the family tree to discover who came to see Ethan at the hospital.

How Holly Grew and Grew

At 6 Weeks

Like all young babies, Holly slept a lot and drank only milk.

Weight	Height
4 kg **(8** lbs.)	**54** cm **(21** in.)

At 6 Months

She could sit up and had fun making sounds. She started getting her first teeth.

Weight	Height
6.5 kg **(14** lbs.)	**65** cm **(26** in.)

At 10 Months

She could crawl on all fours, sometimes very fast! She understood what you said to her.

Weight	Height
8 kg **(18** lbs.)	**70** cm **(28** in.)

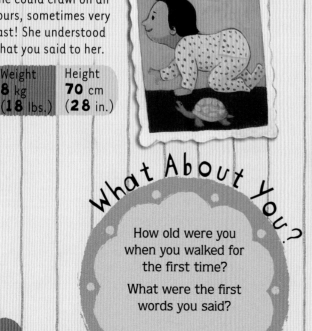

What About You?

How old were you when you walked for the first time?

What were the first words you said?

At 1 Year

She took her first steps and said her first words: "dada" and "kitty."

Weight	Height
8.5 kg **(19** lbs.)	**72** cm **(28** in.)

At 2 Years

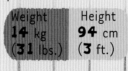

She could walk and run. She spoke better and better and loved to say "no." She started to use the potty!

Weight	Height
11 kg **(24** lbs.)	**83** cm **(2** ft. **9** in.)

At 3 Years

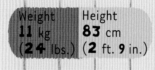

She spoke well, asked lots of questions...and started preschool!

Weight	Height
14 kg **(31** lbs.)	**94** cm **(3** ft.)

At 5 Years

In school, Holly learned how to write her name. She drew pictures, loved to hear stories, and made animals out of modeling clay.

Weight	Height
15 kg **(33** lbs.)	**1.02** m **(3** ft. **4** in.)

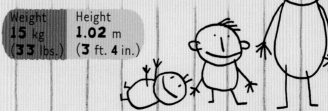

Happy Birthday, Holly!

Holly has grown so much since she was born. She has also learned how to do so many things! She's not a baby anymore. And she will keep growing....

Today Holly is **6 years old**. She blows out her birthday candles. She is a **happy child**!

Cousin Emma is **13 years old**. She is an adolescent. Her body is starting to change and she is growing taller.

Neighbor Nick is **20 years old**. He is an **adult**. He shaves, his voice is deep, and he has stopped growing.

Grandma Katie is **67 years old**. Her hair is gray and her skin is getting wrinkled. She gets tired more than she used to, but she exercises to keep in shape.

Cousin Simon is **8 years old**. He has lost most of his baby teeth. Now his permanent teeth have grown in, and he will have 32 of them when he is grown up.

Ethan is **1 month old**. He holds Emma's finger really tight. He is starting to smile.

The Skeleton and Muscles

Your body helps you stand tall, jump, laugh, and talk.
It's full of bones, muscles, and organs. Ready for a tour?

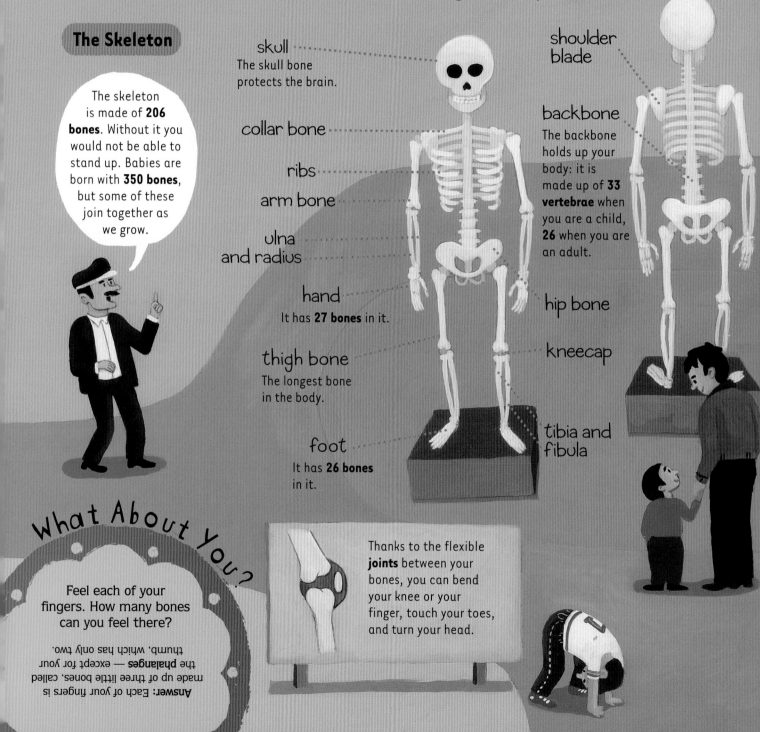

The Skeleton

The skeleton is made of **206 bones**. Without it you would not be able to stand up. Babies are born with **350 bones**, but some of these join together as we grow.

skull
The skull bone protects the brain.

collar bone

ribs

arm bone

ulna and radius

hand
It has **27 bones** in it.

thigh bone
The longest bone in the body.

foot
It has **26 bones** in it.

shoulder blade

backbone
The backbone holds up your body: it is made up of **33 vertebrae** when you are a child, **26** when you are an adult.

hip bone

kneecap

tibia and fibula

What About You?

Feel each of your fingers. How many bones can you feel there?

Answer: Each of your fingers is made up of three little bones, called the **phalanges** — except for your thumb, which has only two.

Thanks to the flexible **joints** between your bones, you can bend your knee or your finger, touch your toes, and turn your head.

The Muscles

You have more than **600 muscles**. Muscles are what get you moving!

biceps

pectorals

triceps

abdominals

quadriceps

Bones are strong, but sometimes they can break. Luckily, a broken bone will heal itself if you don't move it for a few weeks.

The Heart

The heart is a muscle that beats all the time. It sends blood circulating through your whole body.

The Brain

This is the big boss of your body. It helps you to think and speak, and tells all your muscles to move.

brain

nerves and spinal cord
They send messages from your brain to your muscles.

Five Senses to Discover the World

Seeing, hearing, smelling, tasting, and touching are the five senses you use. Your senses are constantly getting messages from the world all around you.

Seeing

With her **eyes**, Holly sees colors, shapes, and things moving close by and far away.

How Does It Work?

Light enters through the **pupil**, the black spot in the middle of your eye, and an image forms on the **retina**. It is sent by the **optic nerve** to your brain.

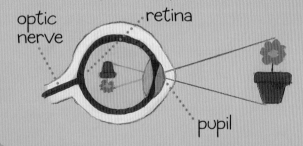

optic nerve

retina

pupil

Nearsighted people don't see well from far away. **Farsighted** people don't see well from close up. Both wear **glasses** for better vision.

Hearing

With her **ears**, Holly hears all kinds of sounds: loud ones like Ethan crying or soft ones like the voice of her dad.

How Does It Work?

Sounds go into the ear and hit a tight piece of skin, called the **ear drum**. From there they are transmitted to the brain.

ear drum   auditory nerve

Warning!

Your ears can be injured by very loud noises.

BAM

Smelling

With her **nose**, Holly can smell good and bad odors.

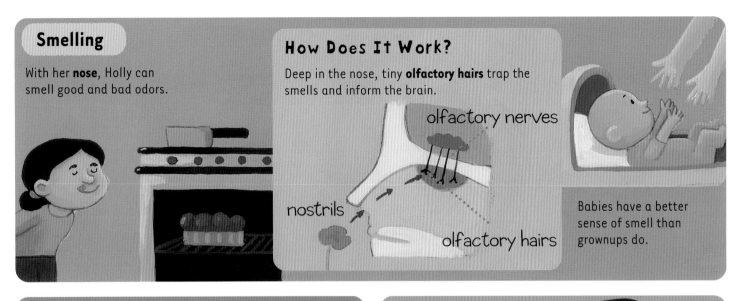

How Does It Work?

Deep in the nose, tiny **olfactory hairs** trap the smells and inform the brain.

olfactory nerves

nostrils

olfactory hairs

Babies have a better sense of smell than grownups do.

Tasting

Her **tongue** helps Holly recognize what she is eating.

How Does It Work?

Thousands of tiny **taste buds** on your tongue will tell you if something is sour, salty, sweet, or bitter.

Your nose helps you to taste your food. When your nose is blocked up you can't taste things so well!

Touching

On her **skin**, Holly can feel hot things, cold things, hard and soft things...

How Does It Work?

Hidden in your skin are tiny **sensors** that feel things and transmit messages along your nerves to your brain.

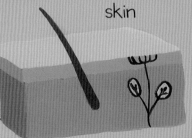

skin

nerve

The skin on your buttocks is not as sensitive as skin on the rest of your body. That's why you often get injections in your behind.

21

You've Got to Breathe and Eat!

Like every living thing under the sun, you need oxygen and food to live. But how does it work?

The Voyage of Oxygen

Breathing

You breathe day and night without thinking about it. That's how air, which carries oxygen, enters your body.

lungs

A You breathe in through your mouth or nose. Air enters your body, and inflates your lungs like **balloons**.

B When you breathe out, your lungs push out air, along with wastes your body does not need.

Blood Circulation...

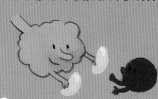

a The oxygen travels from your lungs into your blood. Blood carries oxygen throughout your body to help your body work.

and Oxygen

b When your body has used up the oxygen, the blood gathers up wastes, which leave your body through your lungs.

> When you run, your muscles use up lots of oxygen. You breathe faster and your heart beats faster too.

> People can't breathe underwater. That's why divers use air tanks.

Digestion

A In your **mouth**, teeth and saliva mash a slice of bread into soft, little pieces that you can swallow.

B The pieces travel down your **esophagus** to your **stomach**.

C In your **stomach**, the pieces become a soupy liquid.

D The food arrives in your **intestines**. Whatever is good for your body travels into your bloodstream.

E Waste materials leave your body when you go to the toilet.

When muscles are working, they need **energy**. Blood brings them oxygen and sugars as it travels around your body.

The younger you are, the faster your heart beats: 120 times a minute for a newborn baby, 70 times a minute for an adult.

If you eat too much or you don't exercise enough, your body stores up energy and you get heavier.

If you don't eat enough before you exercise, you could feel faint. Your body needs energy!

Kids' Question

Why is blood red?

Because of **red blood cells**. A single drop of blood contains millions of these tiny cells. Red blood cells are made of hemoglobin, which is red to start with — and when they carry oxygen, they turn even redder.

Good or Bad for Your Health?

We need to take care of ourselves. Take a look at Holly and her friends. Who's doing the right things to stay healthy?

A Simon eats three meals a day, and feels nice and full.

B Emma leaves for school without having breakfast.

C Holly never drinks water because she doesn't like it.

D Jack plays soccer. He loves sports!

E Amy eats candy and cookies all day long.

F Martin spends all of Saturday watching TV.

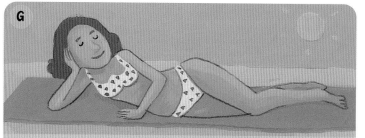

G Julie spends hours and hours sunbathing to get a tan.

H Sarah brushes her teeth after every meal.

I Mark takes one shower a month.

J When he is upset, Karim sits in a corner and doesn't talk about his problem with anyone.

K Before bedtime, Holly cuddles with her parents.

L Ow! Naomi fell down. The teacher disinfects her boo-boo.

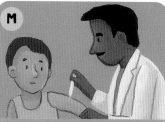

M The doctor gives Terry his vaccination.

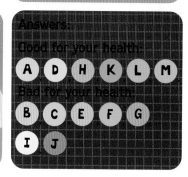

Answers:
Good for your health: A D H K L M
Bad for your health: B C E F G I J

The Healthy Way

B Breakfast is a very important meal. It gives you the energy you need to start your day off right.

C You should drink water as soon as you feel even a bit thirsty. When you perspire or go to the toilet, your body loses water that you need to replace.

E If you eat too many sweets your teeth will get cavities, and you might become overweight, too.

F When you sit and watch a lot of TV your mind turns off. You get into a lazy mood, and you don't want to do anything else.

G You need to protect your skin from the sun by using sunscreen and wearing a T-shirt. Protect your eyes by wearing sunglasses.

I Bathe regularly with soap and warm water to clean off germs, sweat, and dirt that collect on your skin.

J When you keep bad feelings inside you feel sad, and you don't want to play or talk with friends. You could even become sick. Telling someone what's wrong will make you feel better...and might help you find a solution for your problem.

Kids' Question

Why do I have to sleep?

You need sleep for good health. While you're asleep your heart beats more slowly, and your breathing slows down, too. Your body is resting and repairing itself. It is getting stronger. Meanwhile, your brain is busy creating dreams and nightmares, which keep your memory working.

Holly Feels Sick

Disease germs are so small that you can't see them, but they are everywhere. Some germs attack your body — and your body fights back!

The Doctor's Instruments

Stethoscope
For listening to the heart and lungs.

Otoscope
To see inside the ears.

Light and tongue depressor
To look down the throat.

1 Fever

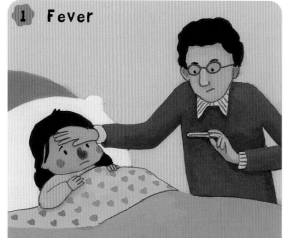

This morning Holly feels sick. She has a sore throat. Her dad takes her temperature with a **thermometer**. Uh, oh! It is 3 degrees above normal. She has a fever.

2 Visiting the Doctor

Holly sits in the **pediatrician's** waiting room. He is a children's doctor. At last it is her turn.

3 The Examination

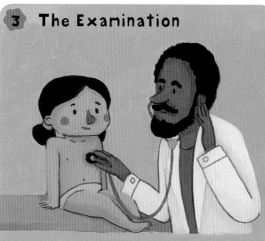

The doctor examines Holly to understand what is making her sick. He listens to her heartbeat and breathing, and looks in her ears and throat. Then he prescribes some **medicine**.

4 All Better!

A few days later, there's no more fever, and Holly is well again. Helped by the medicine, her **white blood cells** have won the fight against her illness.

Inside Holly's Body

A Harmful bacteria entered Holly's body and traveled into her blood stream.

B White blood cells in her blood stream multiplied, and attacked the bacteria.

C They also ordered the brain to heat up the body: that's what fever is.

D The fever weakened the invading bacteria, since they can't stand heat.

What's the Matter?

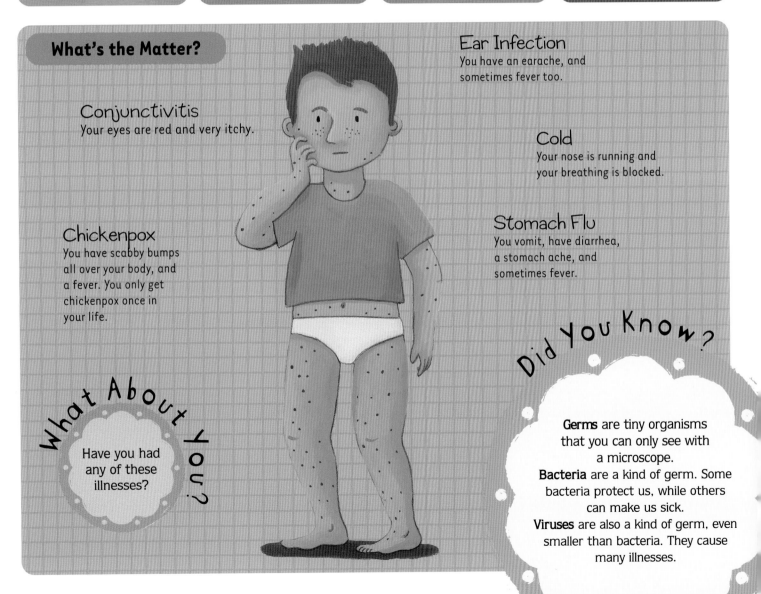

Conjunctivitis
Your eyes are red and very itchy.

Chickenpox
You have scabby bumps all over your body, and a fever. You only get chickenpox once in your life.

Ear Infection
You have an earache, and sometimes fever too.

Cold
Your nose is running and your breathing is blocked.

Stomach Flu
You vomit, have diarrhea, a stomach ache, and sometimes fever.

What About You?

Have you had any of these illnesses?

Did You Know?

Germs are tiny organisms that you can only see with a microscope.
Bacteria are a kind of germ. Some bacteria protect us, while others can make us sick.
Viruses are also a kind of germ, even smaller than bacteria. They cause many illnesses.

Little Boo-Boos

When it is hurt, afraid, or cold, your body reacts and takes care of itself.

**ouch.
ow!
ow, ow!**

Mister Boo-Boos

He's bleeding.

Where he cut his skin, little **blood vessels** are open: that's where the blood is coming from. Soon, blood **platelets** join together to stop the blood from flowing out. The blood dries up and forms a scab.

He has a bump.

Should have worn a helmet! He conked his head! The blow hit tiny blood vessels under his skin. They swell up into a bump on his forehead. His mom takes him to the doctor to make sure his brain is OK.

He has a bruise.

He banged his arm. His blood gathered under the skin. Now it's blue, but later the bruise will turn purple, then yellow.

Mister Noisy

BURP

He burps.

While he eats or when he drinks soda pop, he swallows air that collects in his **stomach**. This air can come out of his mouth all at once. That's a burp.

Aaa-CHOO

He sneezes.

Sometimes when he breathes, dust goes up his nose. It irritates and tickles him, and he sneezes to get the dust out.

PROOT

He farts.

The air he swallowed can go down into his **intestines**. There it adds to smelly gas that forms during digestion. When there is too much gas, he farts to let it out.

Hic Hic

He has hiccups.

When he eats too quickly or laughs too hard, a big muscle near his lungs squeezes tight. Air from his lungs suddenly rushes up into his throat. It makes him *hicc-up*!

Miss Sensitive

Oooh!

She blushes.

When she is embarassed, the blood vessels under her skin get bigger and bring more blood to her cheeks. Her face turns the color of blood—red!

She cries.

Tears keep eyes clean and moist. But when she is sad or feels pain, her eyes fill up with so many tears that they overflow and run down her cheeks.

Miss Weather Forecast

Drip, drip... Brrrr!

She shivers.

When it is cold, her muscles obey orders from her brain to shake and shiver. The shivering makes her body warmer.

She sweats.

When it is hot, water flows out of little holes in her skin called **pores. Sweating** helps her body cool down and stay at its normal temperature.

Number Time!

When you sneeze, air rushes out of your nose and mouth at **170 km (105 miles) per hour.** That's faster than a car on the highway! Amazing but true: An Iowa man had the hiccups non-stop for **69 years and five months!**

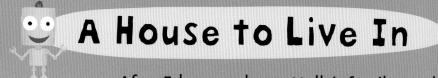 # A House to Live In

After Ethan was born, Holly's family needed more room to live. They all moved into a new house. Ready for a tour?

chimney

TV antenna

shingles

rain gutter

shutters

window

door

door handle

Look at the front of the house and you will see where Holly, Ethan, and their parents sleep. Their bedrooms are all on the top floor.

 Holly's bedroom window has pink curtains with green polka-dots.

Ethan's window is covered by a shade with stars all over it.

Marie and Jason have put a big plant in their bedroom window.

31

How Do We Get Electricity, Water, and Gas?

Electricity

Where's It From?

This form of energy comes from a big power plant. It travels to the house along underground cables, or along cables strung on high poles.

How Does It Work?

An electrician installed wires throughout the house. These bring power to the electrical outlets and light fixtures.

Water

Where's It From?

Water flows in rivers and lakes, or underground. First it's cleaned in a water plant to make it fit for drinking, and then it travels along pipes to your house.

Where Does It Go?

When the dishwater goes down the drain or you flush the toilet, the water leaves your house through a big underground pipe. This pipe takes the water to a purification plant where it is cleaned before it flows into a river or lake.

Gas

Where's It From?

Natural gas is pumped up from pockets under land and sea. It travels to your house through underground pipes.

How Does It Work?

When you turn on a gas appliance the gas escapes into the air. It is lit to make a flame. The gas fire helps you cook meals or heat the house. Some gas fires light automatically (stoves and furnaces).

Others need a match to make fire (gas barbeques).

Who Built the House?

Architect
She drew the plan and chose the construction materials.

Mason
He built the foundation and put up the outside walls.

Electrician
He installed the electrical system.

Plumber
He put in the water pipes.

Carpenter
He put in the wooden beams that hold up the floor and roof.

Roofer
He put the shingles all over the roof.

Joiner
He made and installed wood frames for the whole house.

Plasterer
She put a smooth layer of plaster on the walls.

Paperhanger
He put up the wallpaper.

Painter
He painted the house.

Tiler
He put in all the tiles.

Inside the Home

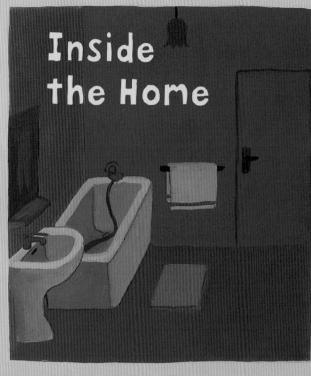

Who is using water and
electricity in the house right now?

Holly flushes the toilet, and has
the lights on in the bathroom.

Jason uses the phone and has the
lights on while watching TV.

Marie turns on the light and dishwasher.

Ethan has a night light on
in his room.

One Day at Home

It is Saturday, the first day of the weekend.
No school for Holly, no work for her parents.

A Mixed-Up Day!

Using clues from the pictures and clocks, can you put this day back in the right order?

The Bath

Holly takes her bath, as she does every night. It feels good to be all clean and cozy in her pyjamas.

Here Are the Guests!

The doorbell is ringing! Holly runs to welcome Aunt Susie, Uncle William, and her cousins.

Number Time!

There are
60 seconds in **one minute.**

60 minutes in **one hour.**

24 hours in **one day.**

7 days in **one week.**

Breakfast Time

Marie slept in. She's having her breakfast. Jason, Ethan, and Holly have been up for hours. They've just come back from a walk.

Supper Time

They have tomato soup, chicken, broccoli — and apple crisp for dessert.

Lunch Time

Jason made spaghetti with vegetables he bought at the market. Everyone enjoys it!

Snack Time

Hot chocolate with Aunt Susie's yummy chocolate chip cookies. What could be better?

Time for Bed!

Holly has brushed her teeth. Marie is reading her a story. Soon it is time to sleep tight. Good night!

Housework

You stay healthier in a clean, dust-free house. Jason and Marie do the housework together.

The Guests Go Home...

Everyone says goodbye to the guests. The afternoon is nearly over!

What to Wear?

Every morning Holly gets dressed. But what should she wear? That depends on the weather and the season.

Autumn

Winter

Spring

Summer

shirts

winter boots

sneakers

rain boots

sandals

tights

socks

leather shoes

wool sweater

underpants

undershirt

Figure It Out!

Look at the pictures to see what clothes Holly should wear to go out in autumn, winter, spring, and summer.

What Are Clothes Made Of?

Wool for warm sweaters, scarves, mittens, and coats is made from sheeps' fleece.

Cotton for jeans, underwear, and shirts comes from the cotton plant.

Rubber for rain boots and the bottoms of sneakers is made from latex, the sap of the rubber tree.

Leather for shoes, belts, and sandals is made of animal hides.

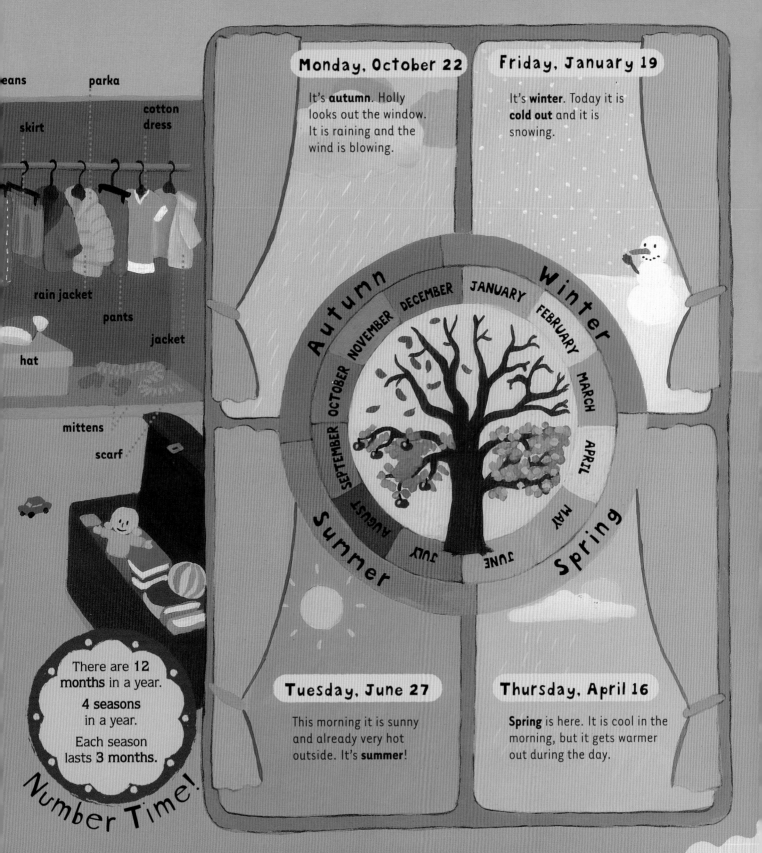

Monday, October 22

It's **autumn**. Holly looks out the window. It is raining and the wind is blowing.

Friday, January 19

It's **winter**. Today it is **cold out** and it is snowing.

Tuesday, June 27

This morning it is sunny and already very hot outside. It's **summer**!

Thursday, April 16

Spring is here. It is cool in the morning, but it gets warmer out during the day.

eans   parka

skirt   cotton dress

rain jacket

pants

hat   jacket

mittens

scarf

Autumn   Winter   Spring   Summer

SEPTEMBER OCTOBER NOVEMBER DECEMBER JANUARY FEBRUARY MARCH APRIL MAY JUNE JULY AUGUST

There are **12 months** in a year.

4 seasons in a year.

Each season lasts **3 months**.

Number Time!

A Good Breakfast for Holly

Today Holly woke up feeling very hungry! She has a healthy breakfast to fill up on energy and start the day well.

Balanced Meals for Good Health

For breakfast, lunch, and supper, Holly eats a mix of healthy foods.

- Food rich in proteins help her grow and make her muscles and organs strong.

- Starchy foods give her lots of get-up-and-go energy.

- Foods rich in fats help her grow and are healthy for her brain.

- Vitamins and minerals in food make her strong and keep her from getting sick.

Holly eats her breakfast without rushing. She enjoys every bit of her food.

Oatmeal has **whole grain starches** that give Holly energy all day long.

Orange juice has lots of **vitamin C** that helps protect her from being sick.

Milk contains **protein** for strength. It also contains **calcium**, a mineral that helps her bones and teeth grow.

Butter has fat for energy and contains **vitamin D** for strong bones.

Jam brings fast energy with its **high sugar** content.

40

What About You?

Look in the fridge, on the table, and on the counter and shelves. Use the colored dots to help you put together some meals with the four important food groups. Yum, yum!

Linked-In Living Room

Holly and her parents keep in touch with friends and family and find out what's going on in the world – right here in their living room!

You can listen to news on the **radio** once an hour.

Television news programs are on several times a day.

Driiiing! The **telephone** rings. Mom answers. It is Grandma Katie. She wants to find out how everyone is.

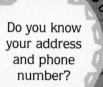

What About You?

Do you know your address and phone number?

Holly has a subscription to a **children's magazine**. She gets it in the mailbox every month.

Marie and Jason's **computer** is hooked up to the **Internet**. They can send and receive **e-mails**.

You can play **discs** and **MP3 files** on the computer, or use the Internet to find information about all kinds of things.

Mailing a Letter

Everything this letter needs to get where it's going is right on the envelope!

A **stamp** pays for the letter's trip.

name and address of the **addressee**

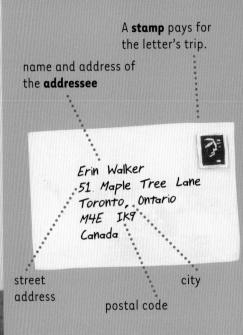

Erin Walker
51 Maple Tree Lane
Toronto, Ontario
M4E IK9
Canada

street address

city

postal code

You write the name and address of the **sender** on the back of the envelope. That way if the letter gets lost it will be returned.

Jason reads a news article written by a reporter in his daily **newspaper**. He reads the paper every day.

There are several kinds of news **magazines**:
• **Weekly** news magazines appear every 7 days.
• There are **monthly** news magazines, too.
• There is lots of news available on the **Internet**.

Kids' Question

How does a letter get where it's going?

First you slide your letter into a mailbox. A postal worker collects your letter from the box with all the others. All the letters are sorted by destination in a postal sorting station. Your letter travels on, by train or airplane, in a big bag. When it reaches the destination postal station, it is sorted again, by neighborhood. The mail carrier delivers your letter to the addressee, along with the other mail for that address.

43

In the Bathroom

Every day the family members all spend time in the bathroom, to wash up or to make themselves look good.

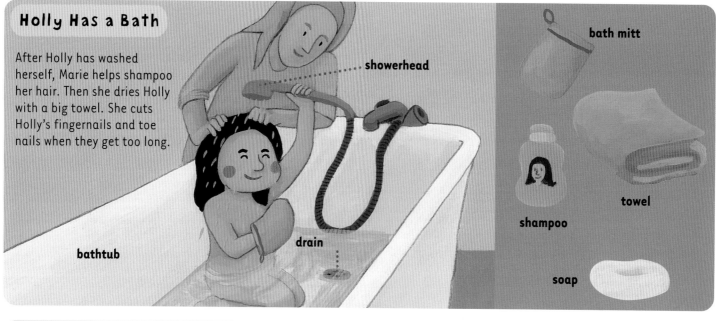

Holly Has a Bath

After Holly has washed herself, Marie helps shampoo her hair. Then she dries Holly with a big towel. She cuts Holly's fingernails and toe nails when they get too long.

showerhead

bath mitt

shampoo

towel

soap

bathtub

drain

Jason Changes Ethan

Because Ethan is too young to go on the toilet or the potty, he wears diapers. Jason takes a dirty one off and cleans him up. Then he smoothes on cream and dresses Ethan in a fresh diaper.

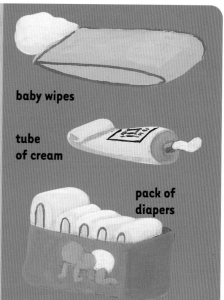

baby wipes

tube of cream

pack of diapers

changing table

Marie Gets Ready

After her shower, Marie puts on a bit of lipstick and eye make-up, then brushes and combs her hair into a pretty style. *Pssssst*, a spray of perfume on her neck, and she is ready to go out.

lipstick

mascara

hair brush

eye shadow

comb

perfume bottle

Jason Shaves

With his face covered in fluffy shaving cream, Jason shaves his cheeks and chin. When he is finished, he splashes on some after-shave lotion and feels clean and refreshed.

tap

razor

after-shave lotion

shaving cream

sink

Kids' Question

Why do we need to brush our teeth?

If you want healthy teeth, you've got to take care of them! When you brush your teeth after every meal you clean off little pieces of food that get stuck there. If you don't brush, teeth are attacked by bacteria that make holes called **cavities**.

Holly Brushes Her Teeth

We should brush our teeth after each meal, for 2 or 3 minutes each time.

1 Holly puts some toothpaste on her toothbrush.

2 She brushes in circles: in front, in the back, and on all sides of her teeth.

3 She rinses her mouth and her toothbrush with water.

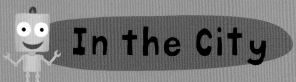

In the City

More and more people live in cities. They live in apartments or houses. They work in offices or at other kinds of jobs, go to the movies, go out to eat, and walk and drive along the busy streets. You can do so many things in the city, day or night....

Figure It Out!

 The paramedic takes an accident victim to the hospital.

 The ambulance light is on.

The waiter stacks up the café chairs.

The baker makes some pastries.

A taxi driver lets off a customer at his house.

Places to Learn and Have Fun

school

music class

library

museum

movie theater

playground

park

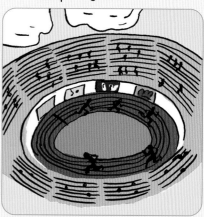

swimming pool

sports stadium

Very Useful Places

store

supermarket

City Hall

mail box

hospital

auto repair garage

train or bus station

airport

Getting Around the City

side street

main street

square

pedestrian zone

bike lane

roundabout

bridge

underground tunnel

All Kinds of Transportation

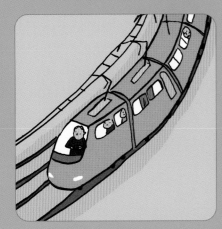

train

tram or streetcar

subway

bicycle

motor scooter

motorcycle

car

truck

bus

On the Street

Watch out for traffic! Whether you are walking, riding a bike, or in a car, it is important to be careful and follow the rules of the road.

Always cross at the **pedestrian walkway** and remember to look left, then right, before you step into the street.

Bicyclers ride in the **cyclists' lane.**

The **sidewalk** is for pedestrians.

Motor vehicles drive on the **road.**

Traffic Rules

Always pay attention to the signals and lights.

Do not enter
Cars cannot drive here.

Red pedestrian signal
Do not cross.

Green pedestrian signal
You can cross.

Green light facing traffic
Vehicles can drive forward.

Yellow light facing traffic
Vehicles drive slowly.

Red light facing traffic
Vehicles must stop.

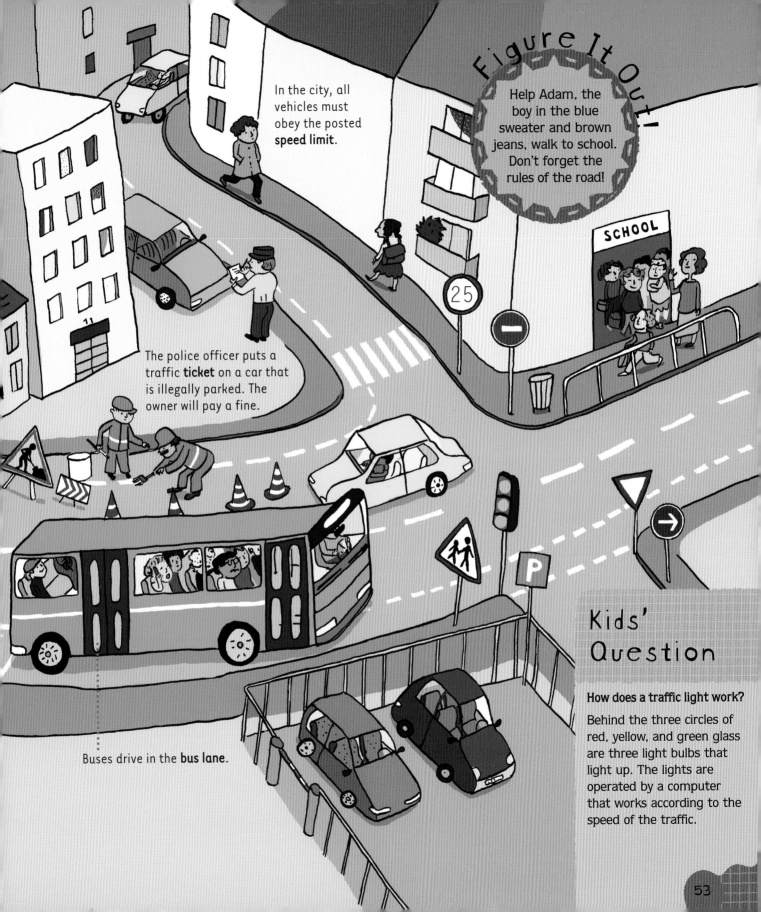

In the city, all vehicles must obey the posted **speed limit**.

Figure It Out!

Help Adam, the boy in the blue sweater and brown jeans, walk to school. Don't forget the rules of the road!

SCHOOL

The police officer puts a traffic **ticket** on a car that is illegally parked. The owner will pay a fine.

Buses drive in the **bus lane**.

Kids' Question

How does a traffic light work?

Behind the three circles of red, yellow, and green glass are three light bulbs that light up. The lights are operated by a computer that works according to the speed of the traffic.

53

A Day at School

Every day except Saturday and Sunday, Adam goes to school. He really likes his teacher Ms. Shone, even though she doesn't let him get away with much! In school Adam and his friends are learning lots of things, including how to behave.

Polite or Rude?

Are Adam and his friends using good manners and thinking about how to get along with each other? You decide!

Figure It Out!

Find **Adam, Lisa,** and **Mateo** in the class photo

1   8:30 Arriving

A Adam hangs his coat on the hook.

B When he enters the classroom he walks by the teacher without saying hello.

2   8:45 Talking

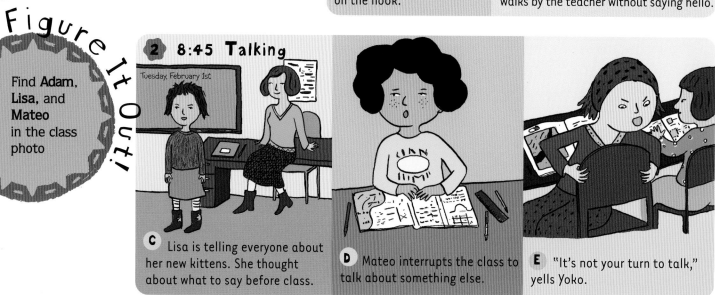

Tuesday, February 1st

C Lisa is telling everyone about her new kittens. She thought about what to say before class.

D Mateo interrupts the class to talk about something else.

E "It's not your turn to talk," yells Yoko.

3 From 9:00 to 10:00 Down to Work!

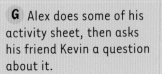

F Every time Ms. Shone gives him a new activity sheet, Mark says, "Thank you."

G Alex does some of his activity sheet, then asks his friend Kevin a question about it.

H Chitra raises her hand to ask the teacher about something she doesn't understand.

4 10:05 The Yard at Recess

I Samuel comforts a little girl who's crying alone in a corner.

J "Give me back my marbles!" shouts Sara, who's lost hers to Cali.

K Mark, Adam, Karim, and Lisa have fun telling jokes.

5 11:45 Cafeteria

L "Shlurp, shlurp, gulp," goes Anna as she eats.

6 12:45 to 3:30 Working!

M When Adam tells Alex his drawing is awful, Alex punches him in the nose.

N Mateo quietly reads a book in the library.

Answers

Following good manners and using common sense:

A C F **H** **I** K **N**

NOT polite or smart:

B *Adam forgot to say good morning to his teacher.*

D *Mateo made two mistakes: he spoke in class without asking permission, and interrupted Lisa while she was talking.*

E *Yoko did not have to yell to say what was wrong.*

G *Alex should have stayed in his seat and not bothered others.*

J *It's not easy to lose. But Sara should be a good sport instead of a sore loser.*

L *Wouldn't it be nicer if Anna learned to eat quietly?*

M *Even though Adam said something Alex didn't like, Alex should have answered with words, not with his fists.*

Lots to Learn!

At school Adam learns lots of things — he writes, does math, reads, and draws. He and his classmates are getting smarter every day!

Clown Puzzle

Ms. Shone asks the class to count how many clowns have hats, how many have no eyebrows, how many have blue noses, how many have bow-ties, and how many are crying. How else are the clowns different from each other, she asks?

Circus Words

The class figures out five mixed-up words that go with the pictures. There is one extra to make it more fun. Can you unscramble the words too? (See answer below left.)

zaptree tarsit

migranster

queenestrine

higtt-erpo kelraw

gglerju

nowcl

Circus Words Answers

clown
juggler
tight-rope walker
equestrienne
ringmaster
trapeze artist

Shape Up

Cali finds all these shapes in the pictures.

circle

square

rectangle

triangle

oval

diamond

Rhyme Time

An elephant once
Lived up in the trees
Until he fell out —
And surprised the monkeys!

The class is writing poems to go with the picture. This is the one that Adam and Lisa wrote, and it made everyone laugh!

Get Moving

Everyone is having fun in gym doing balance exercises. Keep going without falling — just like a tightrope-walker!

Story Time

Ms. Shone is reading to the class. Adam loves this story about a brave clown who saves the circus from a hurricane.

At the Library

You can read all kinds of books and magazines at the library, or take them home if you have a library card.

Graphic Novels

The **librarian** is there to help you find any kind of book you want to read for pleasure or to help with homework.

Chapter Books

Novels

Picture Books

Books of Fiction

Books of fiction tell stories.

Graphic Novels

Graphic novels and comics tell all kinds of stories, mainly through pictures. What the characters say or think is shown in **speech balloons** and **thought bubbles**.

Picture Books

In a picture book you can read a story with many illustrations. There is a short text, and lots of pictures that help to tell the tale.

Novels and Chapter Books

Chapter books tell longer stories than you find in picture books, with a few pictures scattered through the pages. Novels tell the longest stories, and usually have no pictures inside.

How-To Books

How-To Books

Find out how to do almost anything with the step-by-step instructions in these books.

CAKES

Cooking

PAPER PLANES

Crafts

The Garden

Gardening

Non-Fiction Books

In these books you can discover amazing facts about the world. Book subjects include animals, the human body, history, and many, many more...

Volcano

PLANTS

My Body

ENCYCLOPEDIA

Encyclopedias have facts on hundreds of subjects from A-Z. In **atlases**, you can find all kinds of maps.

What's on the Cover?

The name of the **author** who wrote the book

The name of the **artist** who did the illustrations

PIERRE PEARIN
JOËLLE HELOU

BOUBO

NATHAN

The book's **title**

The name of the **publishing house** that published the book

What About You?

What is your favorite book?

Making Music

In music class or at a music school you can learn how to play an instrument. There are so many!

Making Sweet Sounds

Instruments make musical sounds by **vibrating** (shaking very quickly), and then **resonating** (bouncing these sounds against a hard surface).

Your Voice

Sing out! Your voice is a natural instrument, and you can make music with it.

You have two small muscles in your throat that are called your **vocal cords**. They vibrate when you push air through them from your lungs. This vibration becomes a sound by resonating in your throat and nose.

Stringed Instruments

The tight strings of all these instruments vibrate to make sounds.

You can stroke the strings with a bow: the **violin.**

You can pluck them with your fingers: the **guitar.**

You can hit the when you play **piano** key, a hammer hits a string inside.

the **cello**

the **banjo**

the **electric guitar**

And also:

the **mandolin** (from Italy)

the **balalaika** (from Russia)

the **sitar** (from India)

Wind Instruments

You blow into these, and your breath makes them vibrate.

• Some are called **woodwinds**, because a little piece of wood (called a **reed**) is what vibrates when you blow into the instrument.

the **saxophone**　　the **oboe**　　the **bagpipes**
(from Scotland)

• When you play a **brass horn**, your lips vibrate as you're blowing air into the instrument.

the **tuba**　　the **trumpet**　　the **French horn**

And also:

the **didgeridoo**　the **pipe**　the **recorder**
(from Australia)　organ　the **flute**

Percussion Instruments

These musical instruments vibrate instantly...

• ...when you shake them.

the **tambourine**　　the **maracas**
(from South America)

• ...or when you hit them.

the **drum kit**　　the **cymbals**　　the **snare drum**

the **djembe**　　the **gong**　　the **claves** and
(from Africa)　(from Asia)　**congas** (from Cuba)

Figure It Out!

Find the families of these instruments

the **harmonica**

the **double bass**

the **triangle**

Time to Paint

Every Wednesday after school Adam and his friends go to a special class, where they're learning how to make art!

The Color Wheel

There is color all around you, everywhere you look. It is fun to make art because you can use colors in all kinds of wonderful ways.

blue

green

purple

yellow

red

orange

There are three **primary** colors: red, blue, and yellow.

When you mix these colors, you can make other colors! These are called **secondary** colors. Mix red and yellow to get orange, blue and yellow to get green, and red and blue to get purple.

A color can have many different **shades** — from very pale to very dark.

Adam

His medium: Watercolor paints. When you mix these paints with water you have transparent colors.
His technique: Painting with fine brushes. He uses the roller or the big brush to paint big areas of color.
His colors: Adam likes light colors.

paints

roller

brush

Adam

You need light to see colors properly.

What About You?

What are your favorite colors?

warm colors

cool colors

Robert

His medium: Oil pastels.

His technique: Making big shapes out of lots of dots that don't touch each other.

His colors: He uses green, blue, and gray. These are cool colors.

Robert

Claudia

Claudia

Her medium: Thick gouache paint.

Her technique: Painting with her fingers and with pieces of cardboard.

Her colors: Claudia likes red, yellow, and orange. These are warm colors.

Mei-lin

Mei-lin

Her medium: All kinds of colored papers, and glue.

Her technique: Cutting and pasting.

Her colors: She likes bright colors, like orange and blue, right next to each other.

63

Getting Active!

Every Saturday afternoon Adam and his sister
Erin have fun with their favorite sports.

Adam Plays Soccer

Warming Up

Adam runs with his team and does exercises to get his
body ready for the game.

Today Adam learns how to "nutmeg" an opposing player —
getting by the player by kicking the ball through his legs and
picking it up again on the other side.

His Gear

A **team jersey**

Shorts

Shin guards
under his
socks.

Knee socks

Spiked shoes keep him
from sliding on the grass.

The Game

A soccer team has 11 players and 3 to 4
substitute players.

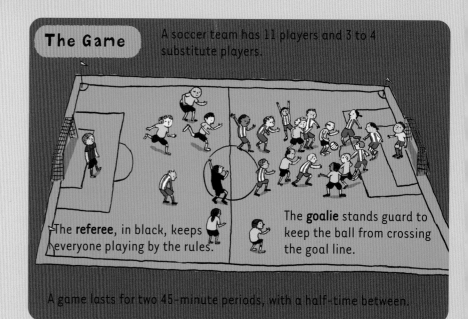

The **referee**, in black, keeps
everyone playing by the rules.

The **goalie** stands guard to
keep the ball from crossing
the goal line.

A game lasts for two 45-minute periods, with a half-time between.

Erin Goes Riding

The Lesson

Halter

Reins

Saddle

Saddle blanket

Girth

Stirrups

Erin gets her horse JoJo ready for the lesson. She brushes him and combs his mane, and then she puts on his equipment, or **tack**.

Then she goes into the **riding ring** for her lesson. Erin is learning faster and faster riding **gaits**: first a **walk**, then a **trot**, and then a **canter**, and the fastest, the **gallop**.

Figure It Out!

Give each active kid the thing they're missing!

ball

judo contestant

basketball player

pointe shoes

kimono

ballet dancer

Her Gear

A **helmet** protects her head in case she falls off her horse.

Specially reinforced **riding pants**.

High boots protect her calves.

Show-Jumping Competition

In show-jumping competitions, horses and riders jump over a series of special fences. The horse and rider with the fastest time win.

Firefighters

These heroes fight fires at all times of day or night.

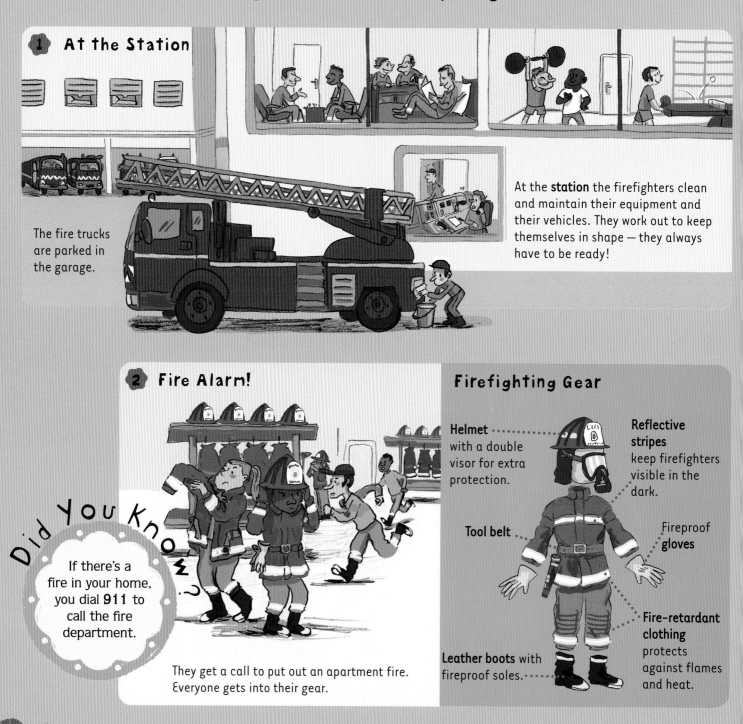

1 At the Station

The fire trucks are parked in the garage.

At the **station** the firefighters clean and maintain their equipment and their vehicles. They work out to keep themselves in shape — they always have to be ready!

2 Fire Alarm!

Did You Know?

If there's a fire in your home, you dial **911** to call the fire department.

They get a call to put out an apartment fire. Everyone gets into their gear.

Firefighting Gear

Helmet with a double visor for extra protection.

Reflective stripes keep firefighters visible in the dark.

Tool belt

Fireproof gloves

Leather boots with fireproof soles.

Fire-retardant clothing protects against flames and heat.

3 On the Way!

The fire truck starts its **siren** and **flashing lights**: other vehicles must let it pass.

4 Fighting Fire with Water

If there's no **hydrant** nearby, a water pump truck does the job! The firefighters spray water on the flames with the **fire hose**.

5 To the Rescue!

The long **ladder** lifts firefighters very high, to help them save people who are trapped by the flames and smoke.

6 Job Done!

The fire is out and no one was injured. The firefighters go back to the station to relax before the next alarm comes in.

Going Shopping

Downtown or at the mall, there are lots of stores and restaurants. You can buy clothes, toys, and food — just about everything. You can also get your hair cut, and even get your shoes repaired!

Corner CAFÉ

Best Groceries

You can get something to drink at the café.

Fruits and vegetables are out front at the grocery store.

Delicious Bakery

The bakery smells good — must be fresh bread!

Tina's Flowers

The florist sells plants and flowers.

Fish So Fresh

All kinds of fish today!

Figure It Out!

Shopping List Help

Chuck, Sylvia, Margaret, and Gary have some shopping to do and errands to run. Help them find exactly where they can get what they need.

Chuck
- Look at electric train set.
- Get a haircut.

Sylvia
- Fill up the gas tank.
- Have a coffee.
- Buy a cake.

Margaret
Buy:
- 1 steak
- 2 tomatoes
- a watch

Gary
Buy:
- salmon for dinner
- a magazine
- a shirt

SERVICE STATION

Joe's GARAGE

The mechanic repairs cars.

Fine & Fancy Jewelers

Jewelry galore.

Fill up the tank at the gas station.

BUTCHER

ant meat
om the
tcher shop?

Fab Fashions

The boutique sells clothes for men and women.

TOYS

Wow — so many toys and games!

Perfect Hair Salon

You can get your hair cut here.

NEWS • CANDY • CARDS

It's fun to go to the restaurant for a special birthday dinner.

Family Restaurant

The news stand carries newspapers and magazines.

At the Supermarket

You can find all kinds of things along the supermarket's aisles. Hundreds of different products are delivered to this huge store each and every day.

Before the Store Opens

Deliveries Come In

- The **merchandise** comes in on trucks large and small. Fresh and frozen foods travel to the supermarket in **refrigerated** trucks.

- The store employees unload the trucks onto **dollies**, and roll the merchandise to the back doors.

- They store the merchandise in the big **stockroom** behind the store. From there it is moved onto the supermarket's shelves as needed.

In the Store

- The cleaning crew washes the floors.

- Some store employees put **price stickers** on products.

- Others stock up the shelves on every **aisle**.

The Supermarket Is Open!

The **security guard** watches at the doors to prevent theft.

At the checkout, the cashier scans each product's bar code with a laser, and its price is recorded on the cash register.

Cleaning Products

Laundry Products

SPECIAL

Tropical Fruit Week

sale

SPECIAL

Meat Department

Delicatessen

Hardware

Paper Products

Fish & Seafood

Cheeses of the World

Fresh dairy and meat are in refrigerated cases. Fresh fish goes on ice.

Dairy

Fresh Produce

Customers do their shopping with a **basket** or a **cart**.

Bananas
Mexico 39¢

In the fruit and vegetable aisle, signs tell you the price and name of each fruit or veggie, and sometimes where it comes from.

Patty's mom can't find her daughter. Help mom find her little Patty! Patty's mom has red hair and is wearing a green coat. Patty is blonde, and wearing something blue. (It's important to stick together when you're in a big store.)

Figure It Out!

71

Circus Fun

The Bardoli Circus is setting up its big top at the fair grounds.
The show starts tonight!

Before the Show

The Bardoli Circus goes from town to town — it is a traveling circus.

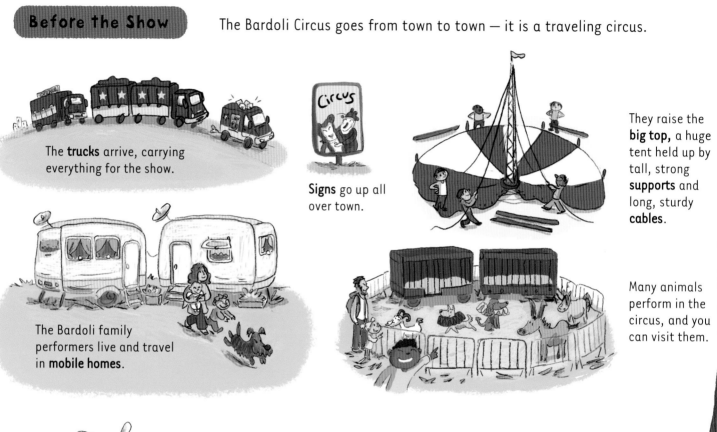

The **trucks** arrive, carrying everything for the show.

Signs go up all over town.

They raise the **big top,** a huge tent held up by tall, strong **supports** and long, sturdy **cables**.

The Bardoli family performers live and travel in **mobile homes.**

Many animals perform in the circus, and you can visit them.

Like all the performers, Bruno the **juggler** practices his act before the show.

Gino the **dog trainer** teaches a fantastic new trick to his loyal dogs. He gives them a special treat when they do it well.

The Performance Begins!

The audience sits on wooden **bleachers.**

Flying trapeze

Stationary trapeze

Paco the **tightrope-walker** uses a long rod to help him keep his **balance.**

A **band** plays during the performance.

The Bardoli family **acrobats** do their act on the floor of the **circus ring**.

Bozo and Chico the **clowns** are comedians, acrobats, and even funny musicians.

Nina the equestrienne

Ringmaster Luigi introduces each new act.

Bruno the juggler

Gino the dog trainer

73

At the Movies

The animated comedy *Penguin Jack* opens today. It's so great to see a movie on the big screen!

Ticket

MOVIES

At the **multiplex**, each theater shows a different movie.

3006

Bad Guy

SHOWTIMES
3 P.M. 5:30 P.M.
8 P.M. 10 P.M.

SHOWTIMES
11 A.M. 3:50 P.M.
7:50 P.M. 9:50 P.M.

Penguin Jack

SHOWTIMES
11 A.M. 2 P.M.
5 P.M. 6 P.M.

Knight Tale

SHOWTIMES
1:50 P.M. 3 P.M.
4:30 P.M. 7 P.M.

SHOWTIMES
3 P.M. 5:30 P.M.
8 P.M. 10 P.M.

You can see all the different **screening times** on a big board.

Sometimes you have to wait in line to buy tickets from the **cashier** or at the electronic ticket machines.

74

It takes many artists, called **animators**, to create an animated movie. After making some sketches, they do the rest on powerful computers.

To start off, they write a story and then draw all the **characters** that will be in the movie.

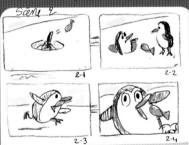

Then they quickly sketch out all the scenes that will be in the movie. This is the **storyboard**.

Afterward, they create the movie on their computers, with color, sound, and music.

In his booth, the **projectionist** projects the movie onto the screen. In each second, 24 different **frames** flash on screen.

You can hear the character's voices, plus **sounds effects** and music, on the movie's **sound track**.

The sound-effects crew use all kinds of things, including their bodies and voices, to imitate sounds like falling rain, a horse galloping — or even a squeaky door!

Figure It Out!

Be a sound-effects person and imitate:

- footsteps in the snow by squeezing a bag of popcorn
- a galloping horse, by clacking plastic cups on a plastic table.

A Museum Visit

At the museum or art gallery, you can see paintings and sculptures from all over the world, and objects from different times in history.

Near every work of art you'll find a small sign. It tells you the name of the painting, the name of the artist who created it, and the year it was made.

A painting of the ocean is called a **marine landscape**. Pictures of the countryside are called landscapes.

You can enjoy everything in the museum on your own, or as part of a group on a **guided tour**.

A painting of fruit, flowers, and things like bottles and pottery is called a **still life**.

Did You Know?

No one is allowed to copy a work of art and sell it pretending it's the original work of art. People who fake art this way are called **forgers**, and art forgery is a crime. You can go to jail for it.

Sculptors

Sculptors can chisel in **stone**.

Or pour molten **bronze** into molds, where the metal hardens.

They also sculpt other materials, such as **wood**.

They can use **different materials** together.

This piece of **abstract art** is not trying to show real things. The artist here wants to say something to you about shapes and colors.

Here the artist painted a picture of himself: this is called a **self-portrait**.

Long ago, many paintings were about **religious subjects**.

In every room, a **guard** makes sure that no one touches the precious works of art.

Traces of Long-Ago Times

Towns and cities all over the world hold clues to life in the olden days. If they've been around for hundreds (or even thousands) of years, you can find traces of the city's history.

The Romans built this bridge over a thousand years ago — in **ancient times**. The Romans built many excellent roads and bridges, so that they could go everywhere in the empire they ruled.

These houses were built in the **Middle Ages**, around 800 years ago.

What About You?

Do you know the oldest places in your town — or in the town closest to where you live?

Archeologists discover clues to the past in the ground. They dig up small things like dishes, coins, and tools, as well as big things like buildings.

This is what's left now of a fortress wall. In the Middle Ages, high fortress walls encircled and protected towns in many parts of the world.

Architects of the Middle Ages built grand **cathedrals** with large stained-glass windows in all the bigger towns.

This fancy building is over 120 years old. Rich people lived here in grand style with all the latest conveniences. They had gas lights, and running water! On the top floor were small rooms for the servants who cleaned and cooked.

This **war memorial** shows the names of soldiers who lost their lives in wars many years ago. It was built so we would remember them.

History

Over time, people invented tools and ways to get around, and then they learned how to grow food and protect themselves. Bit by bit and century after century, they made the world you live in today.

Prehistoric Times

The **Cro-Magnons** were hunters who moved around all the time, following their prey.

Neolithic farmers were the first to live in settlements and grow their own food.

Ancient Times

Here is a **Sumerian scribe.** It is in ancient Sumer that writing was invented.

With her husband, Pharoah Akhenaton, Queen **Nefertiti** ruled over ancient Egypt.

Socrates was an ancient Greek philosopher. He asked wise questions that taught people how to think in new ways.

The **Roman legions** were powerful armies. They conquered a vast empire ruled by the ancient Romans.

The Middle Ages

Sailing their swift vessels, the **Vikings** discovered many countries, including what is now Canada.

Religious **monks** spent their lives in prayer, in copying out books for libraries, and in taking care of the poor.

Knights in armor and chain mail went into battle for their lords.

The Renaissance

Leonardo da Vinci was a genius. He was a painter, a sculptor, an architect and an inventor — all at the same time!

Before Christopher Columbus, **Ferdinand Magellan** explored the world. He was the first man to sail around the globe.

Francisco Pizarro was a Spanish commander and explorer. Because he and others conquered the native peoples of South America and took their gold, he was known as a *conquistador*.

Modern Times

African people were sold as slaves to white owners. Most worked on plantations growing cotton and sugar cane. They were never paid and had no say in how they lived. They were beaten and treated very cruelly.

American and French **revolutionaries** overthrew their royal masters in order to live their lives as free and equal people. The end of slavery followed years later.

The 19th Century

Louis Pasteur and other scientists invented vaccination to control infectious diseases, saving millions of lives.

Masses of people moved to the towns and cities to work in the **factories** starting up there.

The 20th Century

In the USA, **Martin Luther King** and other leaders spoke out for the human rights of African-Americans.

Neil Armstrong was the first man to walk on the surface of the Moon!

Right Now

Your grandparents, your parents, and you — all set to make some new history!

Figure It Out!

It seems that history is full of soldiers and warriors. Can you spot the ones here? Hint: They're all wearing helmets. Why do you think there are so many?

So Many Inventions

Some inventions came to be a very long time ago.

- **Prehistoric Times**
- **Ancient Times**
- **The Middle Ages**
- **The Renaissance**
- **Modern Times**
- **The 19th Century**
- **The 20th Century**
- **The 21st Century**

Thomas Edison invented the **electric light bulb.**

Julie **phones** her friend Naomi.

Brad is writing a story.

Figure It Out!

How many inventions can you find for each part of history from here to page 85? Follow the colored dots above to help you out!

The **telephone** was invented by Alexander Graham Bell.

The ancient Chinese invented **paper.**

Thanks to the **printing press**, we can quickly print many copies of a book, instead of slowly making copies by hand.

At first, **TV sets** showed black and white pictures only. Color TV arrived in the 1960s.

Alexander is playing dice with his friend Ahmed.

 The first **computers** took up a whole room!

 Dice have been around since the time of ancient Egypt.

More Inventions

The ancient Greek **Hippocrates** was the father of modern medicine.

The first **stethoscopes** were made of wood.

Andy is sick. The doctor gives him a check-up and prescribes some **medicine**.

The **gramophone** was the first music player. The sound came out of a horn.

Neolithic peoples were the first to **weave wool into cloth**.

Thanks to the **refrigerator**, we can keep food fresh for days, even weeks, without it going bad.

A **hot-air balloon** was the first flying machine to stay up in the air.

The earliest trains were pulled by **steam engines**.

One early **car** had three wheels and ran on steam!

The first **bicycles** had wood and metal wheels that gave a very bumpy ride.

Did You Know?

You live in the 21st century. The 22nd century will start in the year 2100.

Age of the Dinosaurs

Dinosaurs lived on Earth for a very long time, before humans even existed. The dinosaur fossils we find in the ground help us discover how these fascinating creatures lived.

Dinosaurs were reptiles — as are crocodiles, snakes, turtles, and lizards. The word dinosaur means "terrible lizard."

Like all reptiles, their skin was covered in **scales**. But we're not sure what color their skin was.

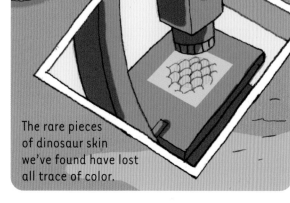

The rare pieces of dinosaur skin we've found have lost all trace of color.

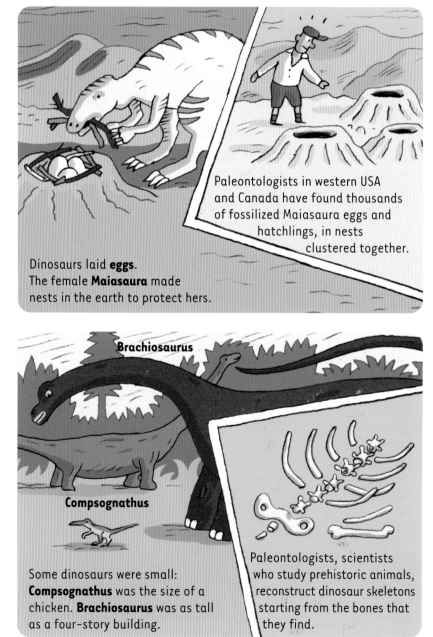

Dinosaurs laid **eggs**. The female **Maiasaura** made nests in the earth to protect hers.

Paleontologists in western USA and Canada have found thousands of fossilized Maiasaura eggs and hatchlings, in nests clustered together.

Brachiosaurus

Compsognathus

Some dinosaurs were small: **Compsognathus** was the size of a chicken. **Brachiosaurus** was as tall as a four-story building.

Paleontologists, scientists who study prehistoric animals, reconstruct dinosaur skeletons starting from the bones that they find.

Some dinosaurs, such as **Stegosaurus** and **Diplodocus**, were **herbivores**. They ate plants, including the first grasses on Earth.

Stegosaurus had an armored tail to fight off meat-eating dinosaurs looking for a meal.

Other dinosaurs, such as **Tyrannosaurus** and **Deinonychus**, were **carnivores**. They hunted other animals and also scavenged dead animals.

Tyrannosaurus had very sharp teeth, each longer than a grown-up's hand.

Deinonychus had a long, sharp claw on its foot that it used like a blade.

Dinosaurs walked on all fours like **Triceratops**, or could stand up on their hind legs, like **Velociraptor**.

Paleontologists can tell how fast dinosaurs walked or ran by studyng fossilized dinosaur tracks.

Kids' Question

Why did the dinosaurs disappear?

Experts don't all agree on the answer.
• Some think that a giant meteor struck the Earth, raised a huge dust cloud that hid the Sun, and caused many animals and plants to die.
• Others think that the dinosaurs could not breathe because of smoke and ash from volcanoes, or that they died from radiation caused by a super-nova, or froze in an Ice Age caused by a change in Earth's orbit. Maybe you'll figure it out some day!

Pyramids of the Pharaohs

Ancient Egyptian kingdoms began along the Nile River about 5,000 years ago. A king called the pharaoh ruled the people. He was like a god to them.

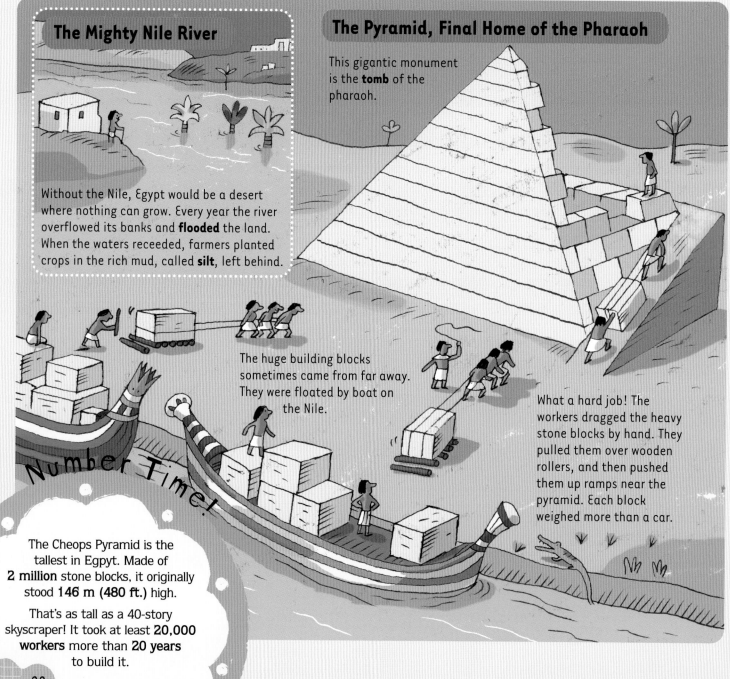

The Mighty Nile River

Without the Nile, Egypt would be a desert where nothing can grow. Every year the river overflowed its banks and **flooded** the land. When the waters receded, farmers planted crops in the rich mud, called **silt**, left behind.

The Pyramid, Final Home of the Pharaoh

This gigantic monument is the **tomb** of the pharaoh.

The huge building blocks sometimes came from far away. They were floated by boat on the Nile.

What a hard job! The workers dragged the heavy stone blocks by hand. They pulled them over wooden rollers, and then pushed them up ramps near the pyramid. Each block weighed more than a car.

Number Time!

The Cheops Pyramid is the tallest in Egpyt. Made of **2 million** stone blocks, it originally stood **146 m (480 ft.)** high.

That's as tall as a 40-story skyscraper! It took at least **20,000 workers** more than **20 years** to build it.

Inside the Royal Chamber

In the center of the pyramid lies the body of the pharaoh.

Hieroglyphic writing and **fresco paintings** cover the walls. These tell the glorious history of the kingdom and its gods.

The ancient Egyptians believed that there was life after death. That's why they preserved the pharaoh's body, and wrapped it in bands of cloth. The royal **mummy** was placed in a coffin, called a **sarcophagus**.

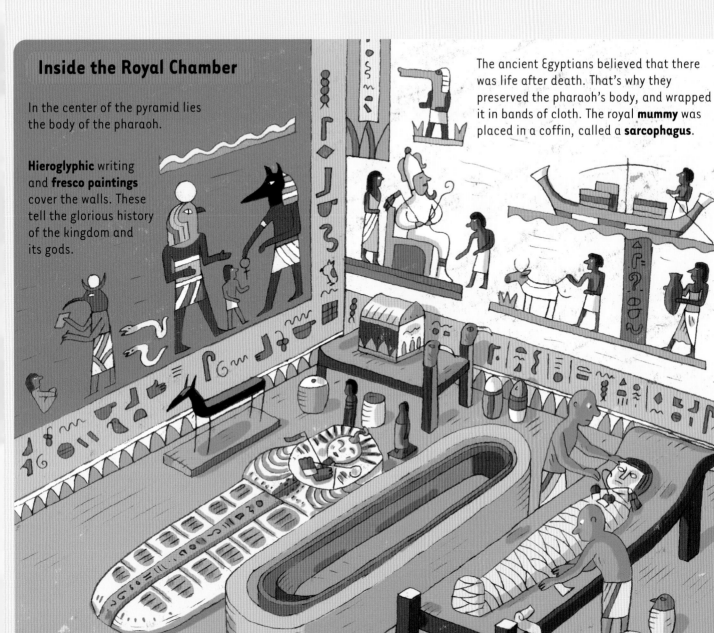

Pots of food, perfumes, jewelry, statues, and household items were piled in the tomb for the pharaoh to use in the afterlife.

Figure It Out!

Find these Egyptian gods on the walls:

Ra, the sun god

Osiris, the god of the dead

Living in a Castle

In the Middle Ages, a royal lord and his family lived in a castle with all of their solders and servants. The lord owned vast land all around the castle. In times of war, the farmers who lived on this land could come to the castle for protection.

The castle was built on a hill, and was surrounded by high thick walls topped by **ramparts**.

A wide **moat** filled with water made it harder for enemies to get close to the castle.

In times of attack, they lowered the **portcullis** (an iron gate), and pulled up the **drawbridge**.

The **blacksmith** makes metal tools and weapons in his forge.

A **merchant** comes to sell fine cloth.

A farmer pays the lord a **tax**, bringing him a portion of his crop.

The soldiers defended the castle from behind the ramparts, and shot arrows out of openings called **arrow slits**, lower down.

arrow slit

rampart

The Castle Keep

The lord and his family live in the **keep**. This is the safest part of the castle.

the **guard's room**

the **lord and lady's room**

the **great hall**:
for eating and relaxing; the lord also holds meetings and renders justice to his people here.

the **cellar**:
extra weapons and food supplies are kept here.

A Boy Becomes a Knight!

Only the son of a lord had the right to become a knight.

At age seven, Arthur leaves his family to live at the castle of another lord. He becomes a **page**, and takes care of the horses.

At age 13, Arthur becomes a **squire**. He accompanies his master to tournaments and battles, helping with the armor.

Once he has reached the age of 20, he is **dubbed a knight** in a special ceremony.

Watch Out — A Pirate Raid!

In 1492 Christopher Columbus discovered America. Very soon after Europeans came to seek riches in these new lands, and began to sail home with gold, silver, and other valuables on board. The pirates gathered, ready to steal the fabulous treasures.

A Pirate Ship

Like many, these pirates are former sailors, poor farmers, and escaped slaves, ready to do anything to get rich.

Their ship is a fast galleon, perfect for a surprise attack on an unsuspecting vessel.

Captain Derek

Pegleg Sam

Scarface Tim

Tricky Bob

Jack Terror

Anatole the Frenchman

1 Ship Ahoy!

The pirates have spotted a merchant ship. They raise their flag, the **skull and crossbones**, to frighten the merchant ship's men.

2 Attack!

The captain of the merchant ship refuses to surrender. The pirates attack, firing their big cannons.

3 Coming Aboard!

The pirate ship pulls close to the merchant vessel, and the pirates jump on deck with fierce yells. Pegleg Sam quickly cuts the sail rigging to make sure they won't get away.

4 The Treasure

In the ship's hold the pirates find gold and silver coins, precious jewels, and spices. This is fine **booty**.

Captain Derek also steals their sails and food supplies. He kidnaps some sailors. They will become pirates under his command.

5 Riches for All!

On an island, the pirates divide up the loot. Captain Derek gets the biggest share. Anyone who got injured receives a bit more money than the other men.

6 Time to Relax...

The men tell stories and drink around the campfire. Soon they will prepare their ship and set sail for another raid on the high seas.

Did You Know?

Pirates kept their booty all for themselves. They were considered serious criminals, and risked being executed if they were caught.

Privateers were pirates who worked for their king or queen, attacking enemy ships. In exchange for a part of the booty, the king or queen protected privateers from punishment.

Royal Life of a King

King Louis XIV* ruled France for 72 years. Called the Sun King, he is one of the most famous kings in history, known for his bravery, new ideas, hard work and love of the arts.

*XIV is the Roman numeral meaning "the 14th."

Surprise Beginnings

Louis XIV came into the world in 1638 after his parents, the king and queen of France, had been childless for 23 years.

After his father died, Louis XIV became the king of France. But because he was only five years old, his mother ruled in his place.

At age 22, Louis took over the throne. He created new laws to make life better for his subjects, and these became a foundation of French law today.

Did You Know?

The royal palace at Versailles had **1,300 rooms**.

The king built a home for old and disabled soldiers, and created a law to protect the forests.

Louisiana was named for Louis XIV when the explorer de La Salle claimed land along the Mississippi River for France in 1682.

A Grand Palace for the King!

Louis built his palace at Versailles. He wanted it to be so magnificent, it took 40 years to complete.

King at Work

The king was always busy meeting with advisers, listening to their advice, deciding on laws, and planning wars to make France more powerful.

He lived in luxury at Versailles with his family and thousands of servants. He was also surrounded by courtiers, nobles, and lords who came to beg favors of him.

A Poor People

In the time of Louis XIV, the farmers and villagers were very poor. What made it worse were the high taxes they paid to support wars the king fought. The lords and nobles did not have to pay taxes!

The farmers' houses were small and dark, and they had little money for food or medicine.

The king had many lavish parties at the palace.

Many children died of hunger or illness.

Annie and Andy: Two North American Kids in 1883

In 1883 most kids in Canada and the USA went to grade school — if they were not needed to help out at home. Poorer children did not go to high school, because their parents could not afford to pay the school fees. Many kids started working at age 12 or 13.

Annie Is an 8-Year-Old Student

Annie is at school every weekday between 8 and 4 o'clock. She gets up at 6:30. It's an hour's walk from her family's farm to school — rain or shine!

Annie's School Things

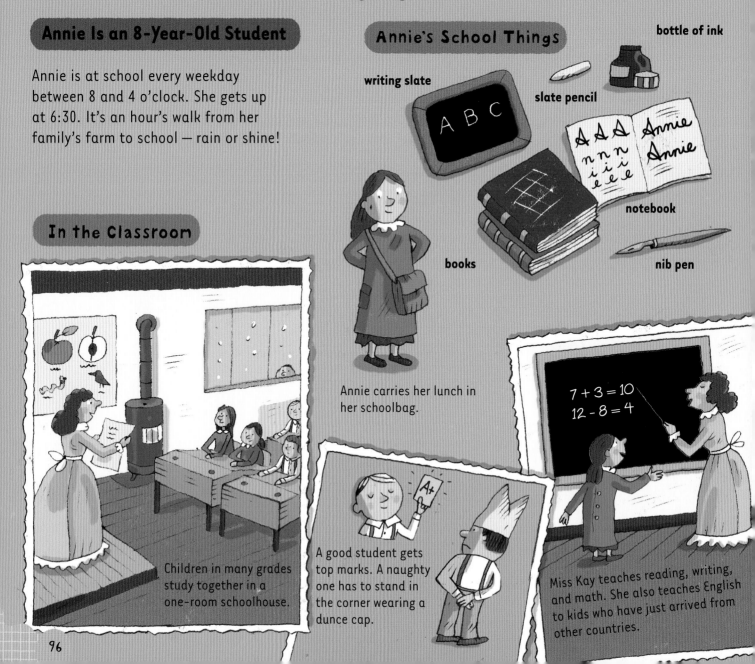

bottle of ink

writing slate

slate pencil

notebook

books

nib pen

Annie carries her lunch in her schoolbag.

In the Classroom

Children in many grades study together in a one-room schoolhouse.

A good student gets top marks. A naughty one has to stand in the corner wearing a dunce cap.

Miss Kay teaches reading, writing, and math. She also teaches English to kids who have just arrived from other countries.

Andy Is a 13-Year-Old Miner

Andy works in the coal mine from 5 in the morning to the end of the afternoon, every day but Sunday.

In the Mine

In the dark depths of the mine, deep underground, Andy shovels coal into a rolling truck.

When the truck is full, Andy has to push it along and attach it to other trucks. It's so heavy!

Coal

Coal is a hard, black rock that can be burned for fuel. It's found underground. In the 1800s, coal heated homes, and powered trains, ships, and machinery. It is still used in electric power plants today.

Andy's Tools

He carries a shovel to scoop up the coal, and a kerosene lamp to light the dark mine tunnels. Around his neck is a flask full of hot tea that his mother made for him. A scarf keeps the coal dust from getting inside Andy's shirt.

What About You?

What's your favorite subject in school?

What job would you like to have when you grow up?

A **pit pony** pulls the line of trucks along the tracks to the mineshaft. There the coal is lifted up to the surface far above.

97

A Better World?

For the last hundred years, people in rich countries have lived better and better lives thanks to new inventions and scientific discoveries. But people in poor countries don't often share in this good fortune.

Medical Progress

There are more and more medicines to fight serious illnesses. People live a long life — sometimes more than 100 years.

We're in Touch with the Whole World!

Thanks to television, cell phones, and computers, we can instantly find out almost anything we want to know, all over the planet.

But...

People in poor countries don't have enough money to buy medicines. They live much shorter lives than people in rich countries do.

But...

We must not forget to talk with our friends and neighbors, too.

We Travel More and More...

We can travel long distances by train, plane, and car. We even travel in outer space!

But...

Cars, trucks, and planes pollute the air, and gasoline supplies are not endless.

We Live in Comfort

Our homes are easier to live in. They are warm when it is cold out, and have constant electric light. We have running water, refrigerators, and washing machines.

But...

In many parts of the world, people live in houses without any water or electricity. Some people have no home at all.

A World of Plants and Animals

From the mountains to the ocean, you'll find all kinds of different landscapes — and so many plants and animals. Nature is beautiful!

The **waves** crash onto the shore, digging out a **cliff**.

Farmers **grow grains and vegetables** in their fields.

The **oceans** and seas are salty; lakes, ponds, streams, and rivers have fresh water.

An **estuary** is where a river flows into the sea.

Figure It Out!

- Dolphins leap to spot food in the sea.
- Seagulls skim the waves to catch tiny fish.
- Deer live on plants in the forest.
- Mountain goats graze in the mountains.

On the peaks of some **mountains** there is snow that never melts.

The mountain **waterfall** runs very fast. As it flows into the **valley**, the water slows down and spreads out.

Look at the small stream of melt-water that flows from the snow-capped mountain! When you follow it you will see that it grows into a bigger stream, then flows into a river that empties into the ocean.

A **forest** has many different kinds of trees. Some are very old and tall.

A **lake** is a large, closed body of fresh water. Often underground streams feed it.

The **river** flows into a **stream**.

Plant Life

There are many kinds of **plants** on Earth: trees, flowers, and vegetables are all plants. Most plants have roots, a stem, and leaves.

Moss does not have roots. Moss forms a soft carpet under trees, and grows on tree trunks.

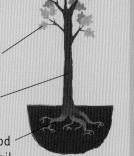

Leaves soak in energy from the sun.

A stem or trunk makes it taller.

The roots drink up food and water from the soil.

Ferns have big jagged leaves, and mostly grow in forests.

Seaweeds grow on the ocean floor. They come in many colors:

green like the sea lettuce.

brown like kelp.

red like the sea fan.

Mushrooms belong to a family of plants called fungus. Never pick mushrooms without an expert. Some are poisonous!

The chanterelle is edible: people can eat it.

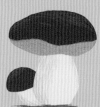

The porcini mushroom is also edible.

This redcap amanita is poisonous.

The death-cap amanita is deadly.

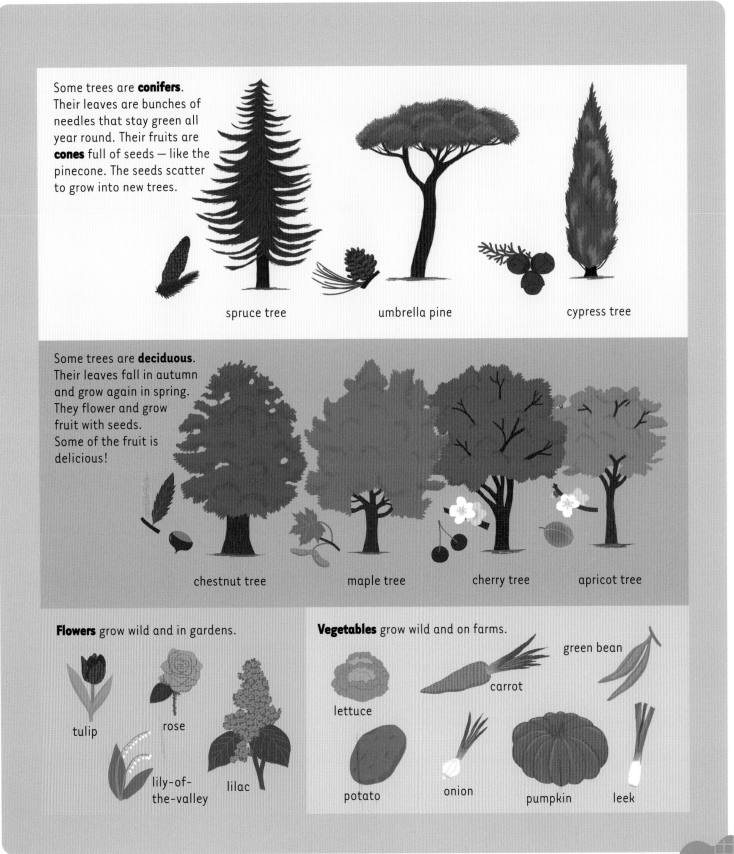

Some trees are **conifers**. Their leaves are bunches of needles that stay green all year round. Their fruits are **cones** full of seeds — like the pinecone. The seeds scatter to grow into new trees.

spruce tree

umbrella pine

cypress tree

Some trees are **deciduous**. Their leaves fall in autumn and grow again in spring. They flower and grow fruit with seeds. Some of the fruit is delicious!

chestnut tree

maple tree

cherry tree

apricot tree

Flowers grow wild and in gardens.

tulip

rose

lily-of-the-valley

lilac

Vegetables grow wild and on farms.

lettuce

carrot

green bean

potato

onion

pumpkin

leek

Invertebrate Animals (these have no skeleton inside)

Insects have six legs.

housefly

butterfly

stag beetle

Spiders have eight legs.

tarantula

Worms have no legs.

Centipedes have from 30 to over 100 legs!

Mollusk bodies are very soft. They are sometimes protected inside a shell.

slug

snail

octopus

Sponges are very simple animal forms that live in the sea.

sponge

Sea urchins and **sea stars** have bodies divided into five parts. They live in the ocean.

sea urchin

sea star

Hard shells protect **crustaceans'** bodies.

lobster

shrimp

Vertebrate Animals (these have skeletons inside)

Amphibians live both in and out of water.

frog

toad

newt

salamander

Fish live only in water.

eel

mackerel

shark

Some **reptiles** live on land, and others live in water. They all have scaly skin.

lizard

snake

turtle

crocodile

Most **birds** can fly.

cormorant

robin

crow

But some stay on the ground.

chicken

Mammals nurse their young with milk.

skunk

rabbit

porpoise

seal

donkey

Pet Animals at Home

Martin and his parents really love animals. They have a few pets at home. These are domesticated animals that are used to living with people.

Fluffy the **cat** is cleaning herself. She's using her rough tongue just like a brush.

Animals in the wild can take care of themselves. But Brownie the **dog** depends on his owners to feed him and take him out for a walk.

Herman the **hamster** is dozing in his cage. Just like his wild relatives, he sleeps all day and stays up all night.

Doggy Facts

- Dogs belong to the **canine** family, as do wolves and foxes.
- Wolves are their ancestors.
- Dogs are **mammals** that nurse their puppies with milk.
- Dogs **bark, growl,** and **yelp.**
- They have a very fine sense of smell, nearly 50 times better than yours.
- Dogs usually live from 10 to 15 years.
- There are over 200 dog breeds. Here are a few:

poodle

German shepherd

Irish setter

Kitty Facts

- Cats belong to the **feline** family, as do tigers and panthers.
- Cats are **mammals** that nurse their kittens with milk.
- Cats **meow, hiss,** and **purr.**
- They can see in the dark. They use their long **whiskers** to sense what's happening around them, and they can hear sounds that you can't.
- Cats usually live from 12 to 18 years.
- There are more than 100 cat **breeds.** Here are a few:

Siamese

Burmese

Persian

More Favorite House Pets

turtle

tropical fish

parakeet

Figure It Out!
What breeds are Fluffy and Brownie? Use the pictures to help out.

Animals and Plants in the City

City buildings, sidewalks, parks, and ponds are home to all kinds of wild animals and plants.

In the spring, after they've spent the winter in warmer places, **swallows** build their nests on top of high buildings and houses.

Every night, a huge flock of starlings comes back to this tree's shelter.

This **plane tree** is not planted in concrete! It is planted in soil that's hidden under the sidewalk. The grate surrounding the trunk sends rainwater into the soil, nourishing the roots and keeping it healthy.

In many cities, **rats** are part of the population! People are afraid of these rodents because they can carry disease.

In the city it's often a bit warmer than in the countryside. Some wild animals like the extra warmth, especially in winter.

You breathe better air thanks to trees in parks and streets. Their leaves give off oxygen.

The **swan** protects her fluffy gray cygnets. If she senses danger, she will hiss.

Lots of **sparrows** and **pigeons** make cities their home.

Figure It Out!

Find these other wild animals that live in the city: The **skunk** digs for grubs at dawn; a **squirrel** climbs a tree; a **bat** hunts for insects at dusk; the **fox** comes out at night.

Farm Animals Moo, Oink, and Cluck

Dave and Debbie are livestock farmers. They raise cows, pigs, and poultry. They grow grains in their fields to feed their livestock. There's lots of work every day!

Feed corn is stored in the **silo**.

Hay and straw are piled in the **barn**.

Stable

The tractor and other farm machines are kept in the **shed**.

Pigsty

Rooster

Turkey gobbler

Hen

Chicken coop

Dave and Debbie's **house**

Figure It Out!

What do you call the mom of:
- a **piglet**
- a **chick**
- a **poult**
- a **calf**?

Find these young in the picture.

Turkey hen

Farmyard

A Day at the Farm

1 Chicken Eggs

This morning, Debbie collects the eggs from the chicken coop. Each hen lays an egg almost every day. For a chick to hatch out of an egg, the egg must be fertilized by the rooster, and kept warm under the hen for 21 days.

2 Tending the Cows

While the cows are out grazing on fresh grass, Dave puts clean straw on the stable floor. He fills their feeding troughs with sweet hay.

Straw is dry wheat stalks.
Hay is dried grass.

3 Baby Pigs

Debbie checks on the sow in the pigsty: she's just given birth to 12 piglets! The sow's 14 teats have enough milk for them all.

Meat from pigs is made into ham, bacon, and sausages.

4 A Sick Steer

Debbie has called in the **veterinarian**, an animal doctor. One of the steers is sick and does not want to eat.

A steer is a bull that has had surgery so that it can't produce offspring. Steers provide beef: roasts, steaks, ribs, and filets.

5 Milking Time

Morning and night, Dave milks the cows.

When a cow has had a calf, she can give lots of milk. We make butter, sour cream, yogurt and cheese out of cow's milk.

6 The Accounts

A farm is a business. Debbie does the accounting every night on her computer before she goes to sleep.

Growing Crops

Dave and Debbie grow all kinds of crops. They grow fruits in their orchard, and vegetables and grains in their fields.

From Seed to Wheat

Wheat grains are planted in the soil.

The seeds **germinate**: A sprout pushes up out of the soil and roots grow underground.

The sun and the rain help the wheat plants grow. Their green crowns wave in the wind.

The Wheat Field

When it turns golden in summer, the wheat is **ripe**. It is time to **harvest** it.

The **combine-harvester** separates the grains from the stalks.

Did You Know?

With just flour, yeast, and a bit of water, a baker makes dough. After the dough bakes in a hot oven it comes out as...bread! Bakers also use flour to bake pies, cakes, crackers, and cookies.

The wheat stalks are rolled into **bales** of **straw**. The wheat grains are ground into **flour**.

From Flowers to Apples

In spring, the apple tree flowers. Bees fertilize the flowers as they gather **pollen**.

When the flowers wilt and start to lose their petals, tiny fruits begin to grow.

Warmed by the sun, the apples grow bit by bit.

In the Orchard

In the autumn, when they are big and round, the apples are ripe. It's picking time! A machine shakes the trees to help the apples fall to the ground.

Apples are good for eating, or you can make other things from them: apple juice, applesauce, apple pies...yum.

More Crops that Feed Us!

Sunflower seeds are good to eat. We also press cooking oil from them.

People like to eat **corn**. It makes good animal feed, too.

The **sugar beet** gives us...sugar!

Olives can be cured for eating, or squeezed for oil.

We eat **grapes**. Some are made into juice or wine.

Small Creatures

They live in the fields and meadows, in trees, bushes, parks, and gardens. You can find these small creatures not far from where you live.

The **snail** slides along on its foot, which leaks slime to help it along. When it senses danger, it pulls itself into its shell.

The **bee** sips flower nectar. Back at the hive, bees turn the nectar into **honey**.

The green **grasshopper** jumps through the tall grass on its two big hind legs.

Figure It Out!

Birds eat grasshoppers. What helps a grasshopper hide from birds?

Ants on the Go

In the **anthill**, every ant has a special job that it is born to do:
- The **queen** lays the eggs.
- The **soldier ants** guard the anthill.
- The **worker ants** build the anthill, bring home food, and take care of the eggs and larvae that will become new ants.

The **spider** weaves a web with sticky silk threads that come out of its body. The spider traps flying insects in its web, then eats them.

The **ladybug** eats tiny bugs that kill plants. Its red color and black spots keep birds away. Birds see these as signs of poison and look for safer meals.

The **earthworm** eats and excretes soil as it tunnels underground. The tunneling brings air into the earth, helping plants grow.

From Egg to Butterfly

1 The female butterfly lays her eggs on a leaf.

2 A caterpillar hatches from each egg. It eats the leaf and grows bigger.

3 The caterpillar hangs onto a twig, and turns into a chrysalis in a cocoon.

4 In a few days, a butterfly comes out and flies away.

The monarch butterfly is brightly colored. On its wings are circles that look like big eyes. These scare away hungry birds that want to eat them.

The **fly** lays its eggs in a cow patty or other excrement. When the larvae hatch they have something to eat.

Did You Know?

Insects have six legs and their bodies are divided into three parts. Flies, bees, ants, and ladybugs are insects.

115

Animals of the Forest

In autumn, the leaves fall from the trees, and the animals get ready for winter. In the spring, nature seems to wake up again. The trees grow new leaves, flowers blossom, and baby animals are born.

In Autumn

The **squirrel** stores away acorns, nuts, and mushrooms for the winter.

The **brown bear** eats mostly plants, berries, nuts, roots, and insects, and a few fish and animals. A thick layer of fat will help it keep warm in winter.

The **stag** (a male deer) bellows. His mating call attracts a **doe** (a female deer).

The **porcupine** makes a cozy den to keep out the cold winter.

Lots of **mushrooms** grow in the fall. Don't pick any without an expert because some are poisonous.

Insects munch on the fallen leaves. This helps the leaves to fall apart and rot into the soil. This rich **humus** is good for growing new plants.

A female **cuckoo** lays her eggs in another bird's nest. When the cuckoo chick hatches, new parents will feed and raise it.

The young **stag** has lost his grand, branching antlers. He will soon grow even bigger ones.

A **mother squirrel** has given birth to four babies in her moss-lined nest.

The **woodpecker** taps his beak into the trunk of a tree. He will use his tongue to get at tasty grubs under the bark.

A father **owl** hunts all night to feed the young family.

The does have each had a baby, called a **fawn**. They all live together, keeping apart from the stags.

The **mother bear** protects her **cubs**. She teaches them how to find food and take care of themselves.

The Life of a Tree

A tree is alive: it grows, it eats, it breathes....
Plants are living beings, like you or any other animal.

1 A Tree Is Born

An **acorn** from an oak tree falls to the ground, and takes root. A sprout pushes out of the soil: this is the start of a mightly oak tree.

2 It Grows

Every year the **sapling** gets bigger. Its trunk gets taller and thicker, and its branches spread out. After many years it is a full-grown oak tree.

3 It Eats and Breathes

The oak tree drinks water and takes in minerals from the earth with its long roots. It turns these into **sap**, a liquid that feeds the tree.

The oak tree breathes through its leaves. It takes in a gas called **carbon dioxide** from the air, and breathes out oxygen. Oxygen from trees helps make the air we breathe.

Kids' Question

Why are leaves green?

The leaves of trees and other green plants contains a substance called chlorophyll, which gives them a green color.

4 It Sleeps and Wakes

In autumn, the sap moves more slowly through the tree. The oak loses its leaves.

In spring, the sap rises again. The first **buds** appear on the oak's branches, and grow into leaves.

5 It Makes More Trees

The oak is 50 years old now. It is time for it to blossom! In spring its flowers bloom and turn into fruit called acorns. Some of these sprout into new trees after they fall to the ground.

6 It Lives Long

Some oak trees have lived for over 1,000 years — since the time of knights and castles! Most live for about 500 years.

7 It Dies

Like every living thing, the oak will die one day. Its life could end because of old age, or it could die from a disease. It could be cut down for its wood.

If a tree is cut down, you can see rings on the tree **stump**.

The rings will tell you the age of the tree! Each ring takes a year to form. If you count all the rings, you can find out how many years the tree has lived.

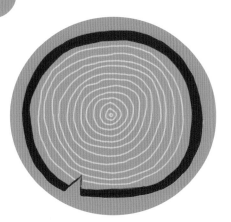

Did You Know?

We burn wood for heat, and make many other things from wood. Houses, furniture, boats, sculptures, barrels, musical instruments, and even paper are all made from wood.

By the Lake

This body of cool, fresh water is home to a large variety of plants and animals.

The roots of this willow tree hold the shore of the lake in place.

Figure It Out!

Find these birds that eat water creatures.

Each bird has its own technique for diving underwater.

The **duck** raises its tail and tips its head underwater.

The **heron** bends its long neck and pokes its head into the water.

The **kingfisher** dives in full flight.

Dragonflies flit around all day.

Bulrushes grow in the water.

The **pike** is a big carnivorous fish — it feeds on other fish.

Water lilies take root at the bottom of the lake.

The **water spider** can walk on top of the water.

1 In the Winter

Frogs are **amphibian**, which means they sometimes live on land, and sometimes in water. During the winter, green frogs often keep warm amid vegetation underwater or on land.

2 It's Spring!

In the spring frogs get ready to mate. The male frog croaks loudly to attract a female.

3 From Egg to Frog

The female frog lays her **eggs** on the surface of the lake.

Tadpoles come out of the eggs. They have tails and can breathe underwater.

Bit by bit the tadpoles grow and lose their tails. Their legs appear, too.

Full-grown frogs have lungs that allow them to breathe outside of the water. But they also live in the water.

4 Champion Jumpers

The frog uses its strong legs to leap into the air. A flick of its tongue catches a fly going by! The frog will hang onto a bulrush with its sticky fingers to eat its meal.

Animals at the Beach

There is so much to do by the sea, and so many animals to look at — especially at low tide!

The Tides

Twice a day the sea rises and falls, first covering, and then uncovering, the shore. These are **high tides** and **low tides**.

scallop **sea slug** **sea worm**

During low tide some animals live under the sand, waiting for the sea to rise again.

Ruddy turnstones use their bills to turn over stones and shells — they're searching for insects to eat. They also poke their beaks in the sand to find crab eggs.

The ocean waves carry seaweed and driftwood onto the beach.

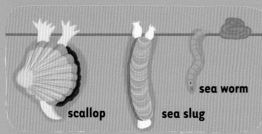

Sand is made of seashells and rocks. Over time they're broken and crushed into millions of tiny pieces by pounding ocean waves.

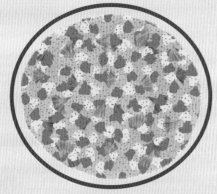

Crabs have hard shells to protect their soft bodies. They walk sideways across the sand.

If a **sea star** loses a leg, it can grow another one!

The wind blows over the sea and forms **waves**.

Figure It Out!

Seagulls fly in the sky, float on the waves, and nest in the cliffs. How many can you find in the picture?

Careful! Don't touch the tentacles of a **jellyfish** — some can give you a very bad burn.

The **hermit crab** moves into another creature's empty shell.

The **sea urchin** has sharp spines that protect it.

Shrimp live in warm-water seas.

mussel

winkle

Mussels cling to the rock with threads they make called byssi, while **limpets** and **winkles** hang on with their large "foot."

limpet

123

Deep-Sea Fishing

John is a fisherman. Every day he goes out to sea to catch fish that you can buy at a food store.

1 Early Morning

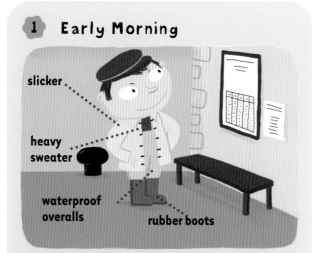

slicker

heavy sweater

waterproof overalls

rubber boots

At five o'clock in the morning, John is ready to go. He reads the **marine weather forecast** posted at the port. Today the ocean is calm.

2 Out to Sea

It is high tide as John pulls away from shore. His fishing boat has **radar** and navigation equipment to help him sail in the right direction.

3 Cast the Net!

When they get to the fishing grounds, John and his crew lower the **trawl net** into the sea. It is shaped like a pocket. The boat will drag the net through the water to catch fish.

4 Catch on Board!

They raise the net and empty the fish on the deck. It's a good catch. The crew clean the fish, then pack them into boxes full of ice.

5 Back to Port

At about five o'clock in the afternoon, the fishing boats sail back to port. John follows the **buoys** that show the way into the harbor.

6 At the Auction

As soon as they've landed, John rushes his catch to the **auction sale**. Here, he will sell his fish. Then they'll be sold again to stores far and wide.

7 At the Store

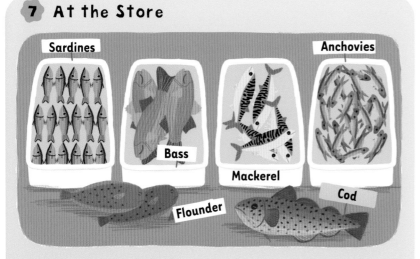

Sardines
Anchovies
Bass
Mackerel
Flounder
Cod

Fish get to the store by refrigerated plane, and by truck. They are put on ice in display cases. Now people can buy their favorite fish to cook at home!

Did You Know?

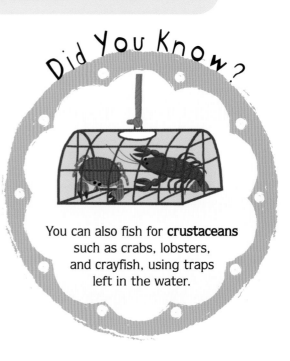

You can also fish for **crustaceans** such as crabs, lobsters, and crayfish, using traps left in the water.

Life Under the Sea

Millions of fish, crustaceans, mollusks, and marine mammals look for something to eat — and may be eaten themselves!

The **baleen whale** is huge. It feeds on tiny shrimp, called **krill**, which it filters from the water with the comb-like baleen in its mouth.

Phytoplankton is made up of tiny plants called algae. **Zooplankton** (tiny larvae, crustaceans, jellyfish, and krill) eat phytoplankton.

Squids eat sardines and other sea creatures, which they catch with their tentacles.

Sardines eat zooplankton. These small fish swim in big **schools** to better resist attack.

Kids' Question

How do fish breathe underwater?

Fish don't have lungs to breathe with, like we do. They have **gills** that help them take oxygen out of the water and into their bodies.

Lobsters hide under rocks, especially when they are growing a new shell to replace one that's gotten too small.

A **swordfish** is ready to spear a squid with its long, sharp bill. The squid sends out a cloud of black ink to blind the swordfish and help him get away.

Figure It Out!

Look carefully at the rocks for some hunters that take their prey by surprise. A **scorpion fish** is lurking, blending in with the color of a rock. It paralyzes small crustaceans with its poisonous spines before gulping them down. A **conger eel** pokes its head out of its hiding place. It has sharp teeth and can catch big, hard-shelled crustaceans passing by.

The **seahorse**, a most unusual fish, hides in the seaweed. Unlike a real horse, it is slow. Fast-moving hunters like eels and squids are its enemies.

Way Down Deep...

Strange fish live in the deepest canyons of the ocean. In these **abysses** there is no light, and it is extremely cold.

umbrella mouth gulper   **flashlight fish**   **anglerfish**

The flat **flounder** changes color to blend in with the sand on the ocean floor. It waits there to catch a meal.

The Dolphin

The dolphin is not a fish — it is a marine mammal.
It has lungs and swims up to the surface to breathe air.

A dolphin usually comes up for air a few times a minute. When it surfaces to breathe, it quickly sucks in air through a "nostril" called a **blowhole**. The blowhole closes tight when the dolphin dives back into the sea.

Its fat-filled jaw and forehead help the dolphin's ears sense sounds all around.

A **dorsal fin** helps it swim in the right direction.

It waves its **tail flukes** up and down to move through the water.

In its beak, or **rostrum**, are hundreds of sharp, little teeth for catching prey.

Flippers help it steer through the water.

Its grey color helps it become invisible in water — good for hunting!

Its sleek shape and smooth skin allow it to swim very fast.

Number Time!

A dolphin measures up to 4 m (13 ft.) long. It can hold its breath for up to 15 minutes. It can live for 50 years.

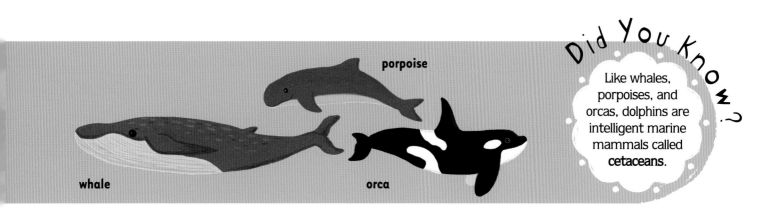

porpoise

whale

orca

Did You Know?

Like whales, porpoises, and orcas, dolphins are intelligent marine mammals called **cetaceans**.

Pod Talk

Dolphins live in close family groups called **pods**. They communicate by jumping out of the water, by touching, and with sounds. They click, squeal, and whistle.

Pod on the Hunt

Dolphins have a smart way of keeping a school of fish or squid from escaping. They surround them and drive them up to the surface, where it's hard to get away.

Helping Out in the Pod

If one dolphin gets hurt or sick, the others keep it afloat in the water, and help it to surface for air.

When a mother dolphin gives birth, one or two other females stay close to protect her from sharks.

They also help her carry the dolphin **calf** up to the surface so that it can breathe air.

The mother spends three to six years with her calf. She nurses it and teaches it to get along without her.

The Rockies in Summer

In July, Jeremy and Niki visit their grandparents for a vacation in the mountains. Today they're going on a hike, and will see lots of new things.

A **mountain goat** jumps nimbly from rock to rock. Its tough **hooves** keep it from slipping.

Mountain climbers climb up the steep mountains, tied to each other with ropes.

Jeremy and Niki's grandparents live in a house in the **valley**.

Before they go hiking with their grandparents, the kids check the weather. They make sure to bring water, a sweater, sunscreen, and a snack in their backpacks.

Niki and Jeremy pick raspberries. Their Gran will make them into yummy jam!

An **eagle** soars through the sky, looking for prey below. It spies a **marmot** with its sharp eyes.

Kids' Question

Why aren't there any trees at the top of the mountain?

The higher you go on a mountain, the colder it gets. When it gets too cold, trees can't grow. At the tops of the highest mountains there isn't a single plant, just rocks and snow.

Another marmot spots the eagle, and whistles to warn other marmots of danger.

Jeremy and Niki don't pick the flowers. They know they are rare and protected.

Peter the sheep farmer grazes his flock in the valley. He makes cheese out of the sheep's milk.

The Rockies in Winter

Niki and Jeremy come back to visit their grandparents for a winter holiday. Everything is covered in snow. It's time to ski!

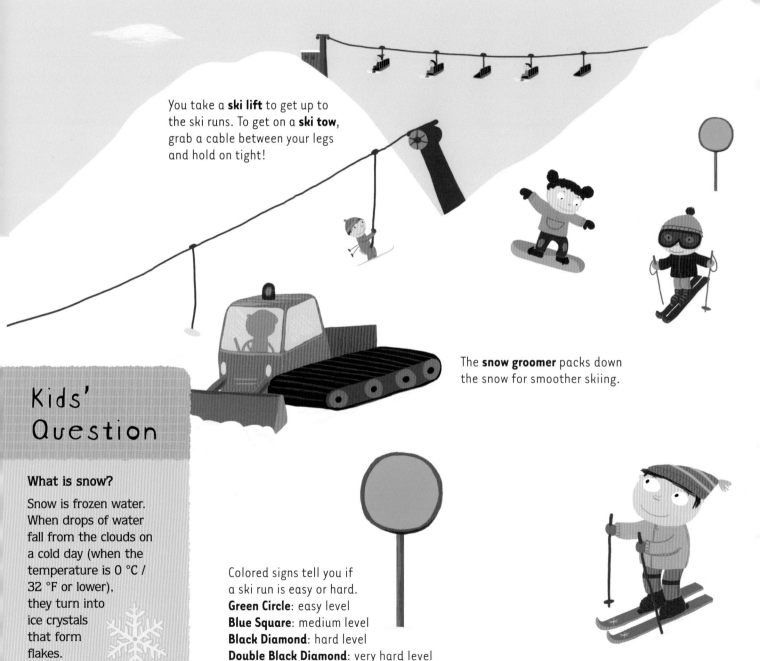

You take a **ski lift** to get up to the ski runs. To get on a **ski tow**, grab a cable between your legs and hold on tight!

The **snow groomer** packs down the snow for smoother skiing.

Kids' Question

What is snow?

Snow is frozen water. When drops of water fall from the clouds on a cold day (when the temperature is 0 °C / 32 °F or lower), they turn into ice crystals that form flakes.

Colored signs tell you if a ski run is easy or hard.
Green Circle: easy level
Blue Square: medium level
Black Diamond: hard level
Double Black Diamond: very hard level

Bighorn sheep have curved horns that weigh almost as much as their bodies. In winter their wool coats get even thicker to keep them warm.

Did You Know?

The **larch** tree is the only conifer to lose all its needles in autumn.

In winter, **marmots** sleep in their burrow.

Spruce and **fir** trees look a lot like each other. To tell the difference, look at their needles.

spruce

fir

The **needles** of most conifers stay on the tree all year round. That's why they're called evergreens! Their thick needles aren't bothered by the cold.

The **snowshoe rabbit** changes color in winter. It turns white to blend in with the snow, which keeps it safer from eagles and other hunters.

A Big, Wide World

Look at these postcards. Where do you think they come from? Some place close to home, or from far, far away? The world is so big. Let's take a trip to discover it.

Europe: the Eiffel Tower

Asia: the Great Wall of China

North America: the Statue of Liberty

Figure It Out!

Can you find all of these places when you turn the page?

Why not start with the Eiffel Tower

the Statue of Liberty

the Pyramids of Egypt

and the Great Wall of China?

Africa: the Egyptian Pyramids

The Poles: an Inuit on a dogsled

Oceania: koala bears

The Oceans and Continents

You can see that there is a lot of water on our planet. These are the oceans and seas. But there is also land. These are the continents where all people and land animals live.

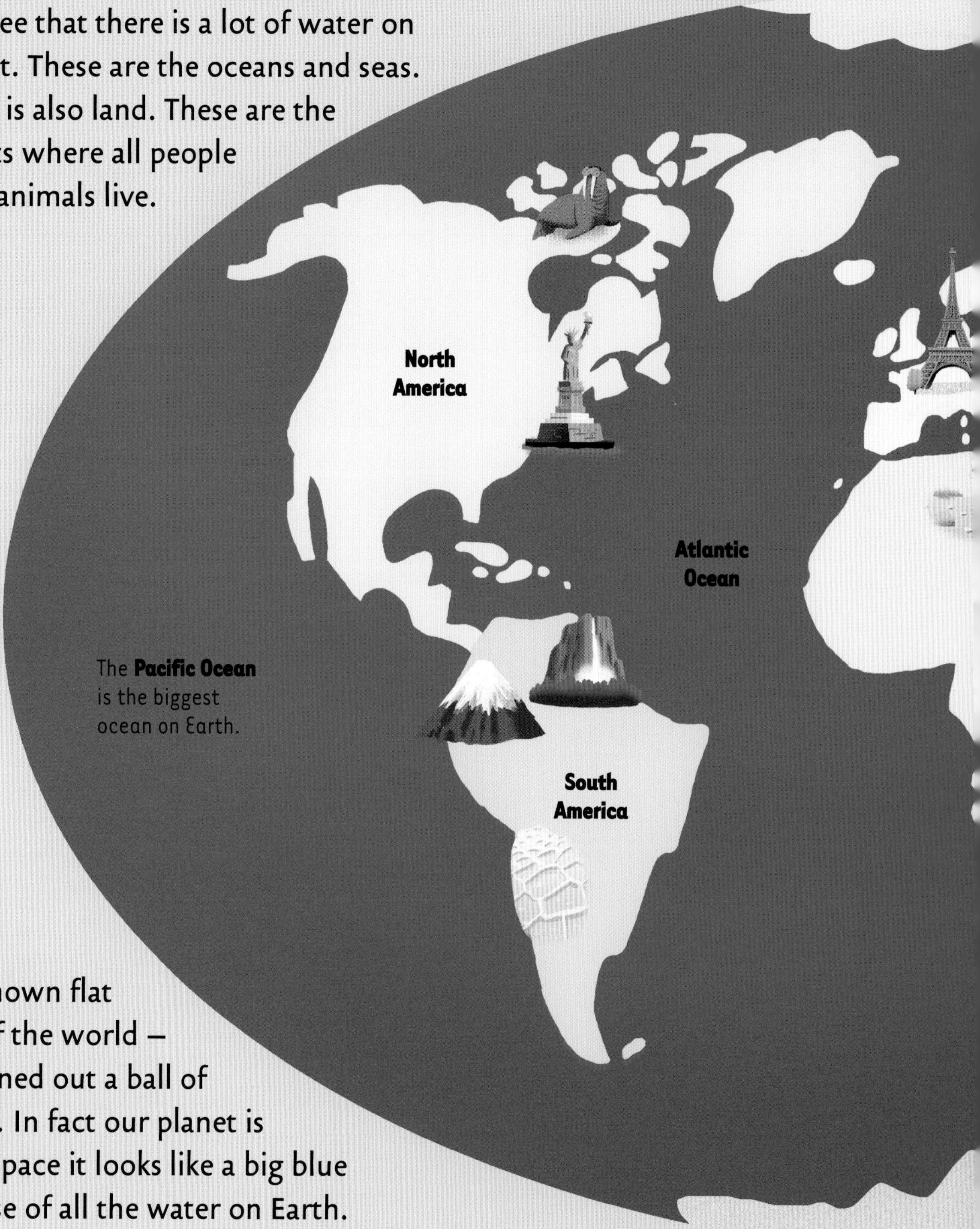

North America

Atlantic Ocean

The **Pacific Ocean** is the biggest ocean on Earth.

South America

The Earth is shown flat on this map of the world — as if you flattened out a ball of modeling clay. In fact our planet is round. From space it looks like a big blue marble because of all the water on Earth.

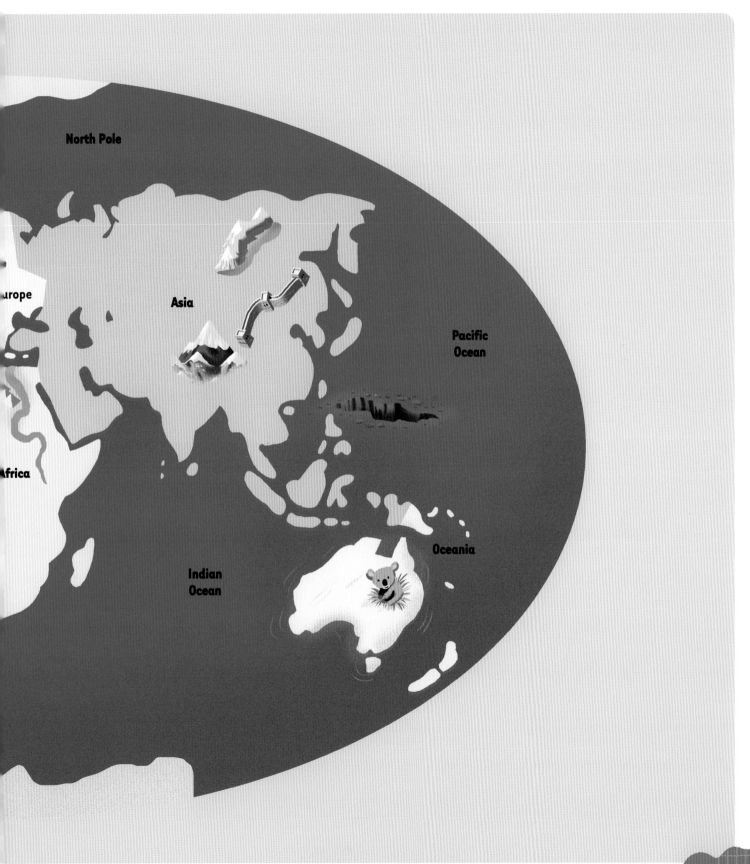

North Pole

urope

Asia

Africa

Pacific
Ocean

Indian
Ocean

Oceania

Biggest, Highest, Longest, Hottest!

From north to south, east to west, from the highest mountain to the driest desert, there's so much to discover. Find these spots on the map on page 138.

The **Mariana Trench** in the Pacific Ocean is the deepest place under the seas. It goes down more than 11 km (6 ¾ miles). You could stack 60 skyscrapers in there, one on top of the other.

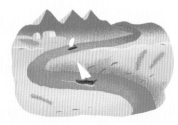

The **Nile River** in Africa is the longest in the world. It flows for 6,670 km (4,145 miles) through several countries.

The hottest place on Earth is the part of the **Sahara Desert** in Libya. Temperatures there have reached 58 °C (136 °F).

Angel Falls in Venezuela is the highest waterfall on the planet, at 979 m (3,212 ft.).

The **Atacama Desert** in Chile is the driest in the world. It hardly ever gets even a drop of rain.

The most active volcano in the world is **Kilauea** in Hawaii, USA. It has been erupting non-stop since 1983.

Lake Baikal in Asia is the deepest lake in the world. It's 1,637 m (5,371 ft.) deep, and it holds a fifth of the world's fresh water.

The highest mountain in the world is **Mount Everest** in Asia. It towers 8,848 m (29,029 ft.) into the sky — as high as many jet aircraft fly.

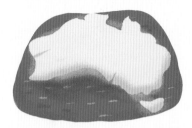

Australia is the biggest island on Earth. It covers over 7 million km² (almost 3 million square miles).

Climates of the World

The climate is the kind of weather you'll find in a part of the world.

There are many different climates all over our planet!

I'm from **Europe** where the climate is temperate. That means it is not often very hot or very cold. There are four seasons in the year: autumn, winter, spring, and summer.

I live close to the **North Pole** where it is always very cold!

Where I live in **Russia**, it is very hot in the summer and very cold in the winter.

We live high up in **Mongolia** so the air is very cold.

During the rainy season where I live in **India**, it rains non-stop!

Equator

Where I live, on the **Amazon River** near the Equator, the air is always hot and humid.

I live in **southern Africa** where it's always hot out.

I live in the **Australian** desert, where it hardly ever rains.

The Earth Is Round

Planet Earth is a round ball when you see it from space.
Though you can't tell, it's always moving!

Day and Night

Earth circles (**orbits**) around the Sun, which heats our planet and gives it sunlight.

Earth is also **rotating** — spinning like a top — at the same time. Because of this the Sun does not light up all of Earth at once.

It is **day** in the part of Earth facing the Sun.

On the other side of Earth it is **night**.

It takes a day and a night — 24 hours — for Earth to make a complete rotation.

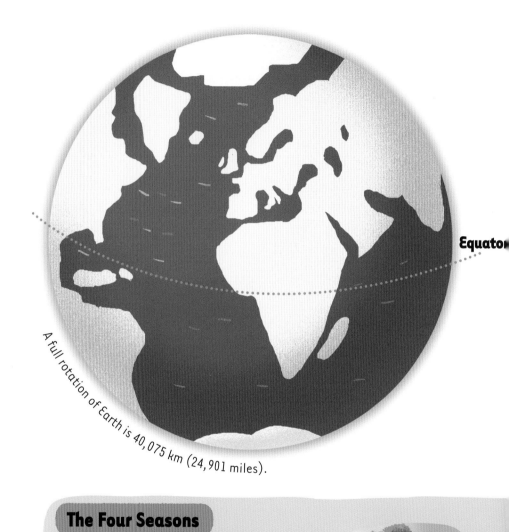

Equator

A full rotation of Earth is 40,075 km (24,901 miles).

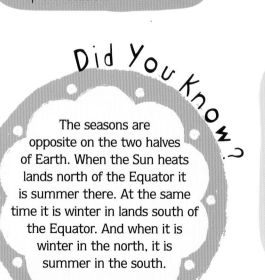

Did You Know?

The seasons are opposite on the two halves of Earth. When the Sun heats lands north of the Equator it is summer there. At the same time it is winter in lands south of the Equator. And when it is winter in the north, it is summer in the south.

The Four Seasons

It takes a year for the Earth to circle (orbit) around the Sun. Because its orbit is a bit lopsided, Earth does not receive the same amount of light and heat all year round.

In **summer**, days are long, there's lots of sunshine, and it is hot out.

What Is Earth Made Of?

Earth has a rock **crust** that is very hard and thick. The crust is broken into a few **plates** that float very slowly over hot liquid rock underneath.

When two **plates** bump into each other, over time that makes a mountain, and sometimes even a volcano.

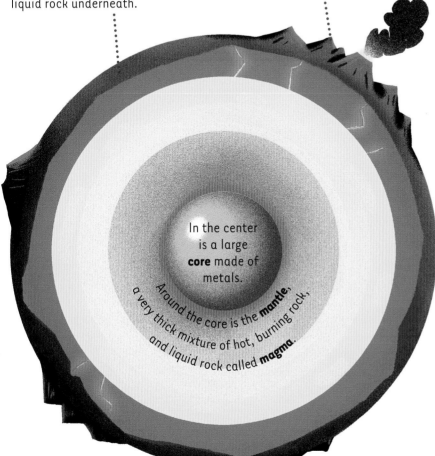

In the center is a large **core** made of metals.

Around the core is the **mantle**, a very thick mixture of hot, burning rock, and liquid rock called **magma**.

In **autumn**, it is cooler, days are shorter, and leaves fall from the trees.

In **winter**, nights are long, there is less sun-light, and it is cold out.

In **spring** it is warmer and brighter, and the trees grow new leaves.

Volcano!

The volcano has been quiet for a long time, but it can wake up...

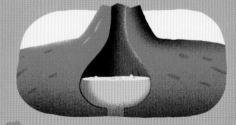

1 Under the volcano, the **reservoir** is already half-full of **magma**, the hot liquid rock found in Earth's mantle.

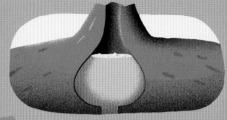

2 The hot magma keeps rising from the mantle and filling up the reservoir.

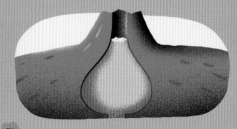

3 The reservoir is full and the boiling magma keeps rising into the **chimney** of the volcano.

4 The magma flows right up to the top. There's a volcanic eruption, and searing streams of **lava** flow down the volcano.

The People's Planet

There are about 7 billion people living on Earth — that's a lot!
We live on five continents, in 194 countries, and we speak
many different languages.

Each continent is divided into pieces like a puzzle.
These are the **countries**. **Borders** mark the
boundary lines between one country and another.

There are over 6,000 languages in the world.
Here's how to say hello in a few of them.

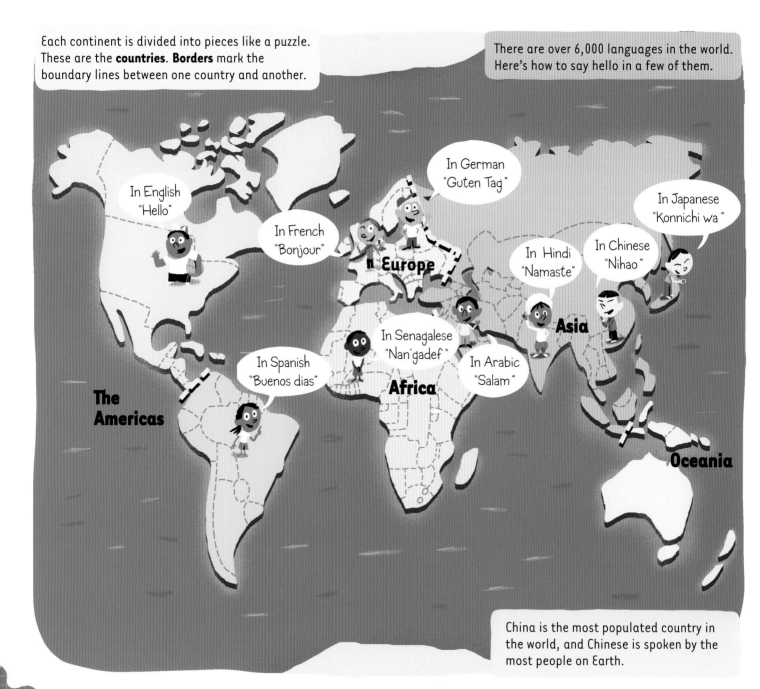

In English
"Hello"

In French
"Bonjour"

In German
"Guten Tag"

In Japanese
"Konnichi wa"

In Hindi
"Namaste"

In Chinese
"Nihao"

Europe

Asia

In Senagalese
"Nan'gadef"

In Arabic
"Salam"

In Spanish
"Buenos dias"

Africa

**The
Americas**

Oceania

China is the most populated country in
the world, and Chinese is spoken by the
most people on Earth.

Houses of the World

Long ago, most people lived in villages in the countryside. Today lots of people live in big cities, too.

U.S. cities were the first to have huge, tall apartment buildings called **skyscrapers**.

Figure It Out!

Every country in the world has its own flag. The Canadian flag has a maple leaf. The flag of Japan shows the rising sun. The flag of Papua New Guinea has a bird of paradise. The U.S. flag has stars and stripes. Which is which here? Can you find the flag of your ancestors in a book or online?

In England, people built sturdy homes out of red brick.

In Ghana, villagers live in round **huts** made of mud and straw.

Just a Roof

Many people in the world have very little to live on, and their homes don't have water or electricity.

In the islands of Oceania, houses often have bamboo walls, and roofs made of palm leaves.

In Cambodia, village houses are built on wooden **stilts** to avoid flooding.

A Look at Africa

In Africa, lions, giraffes, and other animals roam the savannahs, and there's also dry desert and tropical rainforest. It's hot all over this continent!

The **Sahara Desert** is the biggest desert in the world. There are few plants to be seen. It's sandy, rocky, very hot, and very dry, as there's almost no rain.

The **pharaohs of ancient Egypt** were buried thousands of years ago in pyramids you can still see today.

Nairobi is the capital city of Kenya. Right near modern buildings and fancy shops, you can find unpaved streets and slums.

In the hot, humid, green regions where it rains a lot, people gather the fruit of the **cocoa trees**. The cocoa beans are bought by companies, who make chocolate out of them.

Mount Kilimanjaro is the highest place in Africa. Its peak is covered in snow.

The tropical **rainforests** are very dense. The last **gorillas** live in mountain areas here.

Figure It Out!

On this map, find Mariam, Londiwe, Malik, Yapoyo, Yasmine, and Yasser from page 145 (opposite).

Children of Africa

Mariam lives in Burkina Faso. Her parents grow **sorghum**, a grain they make into porridge and other dishes. They have little water, and no money to buy a tractor.

Londiwe lives in South Africa. She has an eye infection, but there is no doctor in her village to cure her. Luckily, a hospital-train crosses the country to take care of the poor people in the countryside.

Malik lives in Dakar, a big city in Senegal. In the crowded streets there are people, goats, dogs, cars, and bicycles. When the bus fills up, he hangs on behind.

Yapoyo lives in Tanzania and belongs to the **Masai** tribe. Her head is shaved, because Masai women don't grow their hair. Men dye their short hair red, or grow braids.

Yasmine is a **Tuareg** girl who lives in the Sahara Desert. Her parents lead camel caravans. They are nomads, moving with the caravans wherever they travel.

Yasser lives in an apartment in Cairo, the biggest city in Egypt. His school is crowded, and there are not enough teachers. Yasser goes to school in the mornings, to leave room for other students in the afternoons.

In the Savannah

Africa has a long, hot, dry season, and a short rainy season. In the evening when it is cooler, many wild animals gather to drink at watering holes in the grassy savannah.

Gnus travel across the savannah in huge herds.

The **baobob** tree is very big. Its large trunk fills with water during the rainy season, and this keeps it alive over the dry season.

The **giraffe's** long neck helps it to eat leaves off tree branches.

Zebras live in herds. Their stripes help to camouflage them in the long grasses.

Hidden in the grasses, a **leopard** stalks its prey, approaching silently.

When **antelopes** come to drink at the watering hole, they stay alert so that they can quickly escape if a predator attacks.

Figure It Out!

How many giraffes, elephants, antelopes, zebras, and gnus can you count near the watering hole?

An **elephant** uses its trunk to suck up water. Adult elephants are so big that no animal dares attack.

Sharing Dinner

Some animals like leopards eat meat. They are called **carnivores.** Other animals, like antelopes, eat plants. They are called **herbivores.** When a herbivore is killed it becomes a meal for many carnivores.

1

A young antelope did not see the leopard attacking him, as fast as a car on the highway! Now he's trying to get away. He's fast, but not as fast as his hunter.

2

The leopard brought down the antelope, but he's very tired from the hunt. While he starts to eat, hyenas gather, yelping.

3

The **hyenas** have chased away the leopard and are feasting. A hyena's jaw is stronger than a crocodile's.

4

The hyenas have eaten all they want. The next day it is the **vultures'** turn to make a meal of the remains.

5

When nothing is left but bones, **insects** finish cleaning the skeleton.

Lion, King of the Beasts

Lions belong to the cat family — along with tigers and house cats! They are the strongest of the African carnivores. Lions live in groups called prides, which include two or three males and ten or so females and their cubs.

Male lions have a thick **mane** of fur that begins to grow when they are about three years old.

A long **tail** is useful for brushing away biting insects.

The lion's tawny **fur** (in shades of gold to brown) makes it hard to spot among the dried grasses of the savannah.

Lions are carnivores, and their big, sharp **teeth** help them catch and kill their prey quickly.

Number Time!

Male lions can be more then 2 m (6 ft.) long and 1.2 m (3.5 ft.) tall. They can weigh between 150 to 250 kg (254–423 lbs.). A lioness is pregnant for just under four months. Lion cubs leave the pride at about two years of age.

Thanks to their powerful **paws** and legs, lions can run very fast — almost as fast as a car on the highway.

Lions on the Hunt

Most often it is the females who hunt to feed the pride. When night falls, the lionesses silently set out in search of gnus, antelopes, and zebras.

The lionesses spot a weak animal and chase it down. They form a circle around it to keep it from getting away.

The male lion eats first! Then the lionesses get to have a meal, and the cubs feed last. A lion can eat up to 40 kg (68 lbs.) of meat a day. But lions will often go many days without any food at all.

Sometimes the male lion goes out to hunt by himself. The hunt is very tiring, and that's why lions can sleep the whole day away!

Lion mothers help each other out. While some mothers are away hunting, other mothers take care of their cubs and nurse them with milk.

Kids' Question

Are lions cruel animals?

Lions kill other animals so that they can eat. If they did not hunt, they would not survive! And lions are useful in the savannah. They most often chase old or sick animals who can't keep up with the herd. These animals would die soon anyway. And because of a chemical released in their bodies during the chase, they don't feel much pain.

149

A Look at the Americas

The American continent is gigantic! It stretches all the way from the North Pole at the top to the South Pole at the bottom. There are cities crowded with millions of people, and there are also places few have ever seen.

You can find many big lakes and forests across **Canada**. Parts of it are at the very top of the world!

You can find the Statue of Liberty in **New York**, in the United States. It is a big metal statue that was a gift from France.

People farm vast fields of wheat with huge machines on the plains of the **United States** and **Canada.**

La Paz is the capital city of Bolivia. It is the highest city in the world!

Did You Know?

Most Canadians speak English, and some speak French. Children across the country learn both languages in school. They also learn two versions of the national anthem "O Canada," one with English words, and one with French words.

Ushuaia, in Argentina, is the southernmost city on our planet.

Every year, the people of **Rio de Janeiro** in Brazil have a big festival called the Carnaval. The famous music and dancing parades go on for days.

Children of the Americas

Timun is an Inuit boy. He lives in Alaska, in a red house. He builds igloos with his friends for fun. Long ago, the Inuit lived in igloos during the winter. Now they build them for winter hunting far from home.

Alice lives in Quebec City, one of the oldest cities in the Americas. This Canadian city is over 400 years old. The French explorer Samuel de Champlain founded it in 1608. Now many of the people here are related to French settlers who came long ago.

Keisha lives in New York. People from all over move here to make a better life. Keisha wants to be a sports star in this great big city!

Tani lives in Brazil, along the Amazon River. She belongs to the Baniwa tribe. Her house has no windows, so she sleeps in her hammock with a mosquito net.

Juan lives in the high mountains of Ecuador. In the mornings he goes to school. After lunch he helps his family, weaving carpets on a hand loom.

Marco lives in Rio de Janeiro, a big city in Brazil. He loves playing soccer, the national sport!

In the Amazon Rainforest

In Brazil, the mighty Amazon River winds its way through the biggest forest in the world. This hot, wet rainforest is a true paradise for many amazing animals.

The forest **canopy** is the tops of the tallest trees, 60 m (180 ft.) in the air. It's as high up as a 16-story building! Up here, bright flowers blossom in full sunlight.

The **under canopy** has less sunlight. Vines curl themselves around tree branches and trunks.

The **forest floor** is covered in dead wood and tree roots. Because it is very shady here, only ferns and shrubs grow well. But tall trees start out here too — as skinny saplings!

The **sloth** creeps among the trees very slowly, hanging onto tree branches. It is so slow that fungi grow on its fur, and turn it green!

The **leopard** knows how to climb up trees to catch a sloth.

The **tapir** pushes plants and leaves into its mouth with its long nose.

The **armadillo** rolls into a ball when it senses danger.

How many butterflies, lizards, and frogs can you find in the forest?

Macaws have brilliant feathers. Their rasping cries ring through the rainforest.

The **toucan** has a huge, very colorful bill.

The **pygmy marmoset** is the smallest monkey — barely bigger than a mouse. It lives hidden in the trees.

Poison dart frogs are brightly colored. But watch out hunters, their skin is poisonous.

During the rainy season the forest floor is **flooded**.

The **anaconda** is the biggest snake in the world. It slithers through the water to find a meal.

Piranha fish have needle-sharp teeth, and eat meat.

The **Goliath Bird Eater tarantula** does not actually eat birds. But it is the largest spider in the world and can eat a mouse!

The **giant anteater** feeds on ants that it catches with its long, sticky tongue.

A Look at Asia

Asia is the largest continent on Earth. It is also the most populated continent, with almost 4 billion people living there!

The **Trans-Siberian** train crosses Asia. It is the longest railroad in the world.

Saudi Arabia has lots of petroleum. Giant ships carry it to countries all over the world. Petroleum is what makes cars and planes go!

Mount Everest — the highest in the world!

Mount Fuji is very special to the Japanese. It is the highest point in Japan.

The **Great Wall of China** protected the ancient Chinese from invasion.

The **Taj Mahal** is a famous old palace in India.

People in **Asia** eat a lot of **rice**. Farmers grow it in flooded fields.

Cows are sacred to the Hindus in **India**. No one may harm them.

Did You Know?

There are many different kinds of writing in Asia. In Russia, they use the Cyrillic alphabet. Доброе утро.

You read Arabic writing from right to left. صباح الخير.

Chinese writing uses characters that look like little drawings. 你好

Children of Asia

Sunita lives in a small village house in India. She has no bathroom — so to bathe, she tips a bucket of water over her head.

Durzu is from Mongolia. His family lives in a big, round tent called a **yurt**. His parents raise camels, horses, and sheep.

Yoko lives in Japan. In her house, you take off your shoes before you walk on the straw **tatami** mats that cover the floor.

Gok-chi lives in China near the city of Beijing. Like many Chinese kids, he does not have brothers or sisters. Familes need to be small so that everyone has enough.

Alexandra lives in Siberia, a huge region in Russia. Winters there are very cold!

Shireen lives in Iran. Her family is Muslim. When she goes out she wears a white headscarf, and her mother wears a long robe called a **chador**.

In the Desert

Deserts are places where it almost never rains. The heat and dryness make life very hard. Desert plants and animals use the cool night to help them survive.

During the day, the sand of the Sahara Desert becomes burning hot.

At night the temperature goes down and the sand gets cool.

Desert **plants** have thick, waxy skin that helps them keep moisture inside.

At night the plants' many roots soak up the tiniest bit of water.

During the day the **scorpion** shelters from the sun under a rock.

It comes out at night to hunt, and kills its prey with a poison stinger.

A **jerboa** spends the day in its cool, dark den.

At night it looks for seeds to eat, and gets some water from seeds, too.

The **fennec fox** has big ears, which help it to let out body heat.

It hunts at night, listening for the sounds of its prey on the sand.

A **camel** can walk for days in the desert without drinking a drop. Its hump full of fat gives it the strength it needs.

It rests at night. During sand storms, the camel's **nostrils** shut tight to keep sand out.

Deserts of the World

There are many kinds of deserts on Earth.

The **Gobi** in Asia is a cold desert. It is swept by frosty Arctic winds at times. During the cold season, the camels of the Gobi Desert might go for a month without water. Their long, thick fur keeps them warm.

Death Valley in North America is a flat, salt desert. This is home to the deadly rattlesnake, which hides to surprise its prey. When it feels threatened, it rattles its tail to say "stay away!"

The **Atacama Desert** in South America is very rocky. It is the driest desert in the world.

Water in the Desert

After the smallest rainfall, the desert blooms with green plants and flowers.

When there is a pool of water in the desert, it is called an **oasis**. People have planted shady **palm trees** around Sahara Desert oases.

Kids' Question

Do people live in the desert?

Nomadic people have learned how to survive in the desert. Nomads travel the desert, looking for plants their flocks can graze on, and oases where they can stop.

A Look at Oceania

Oceania is a small continent made up of thousands of islands. Australia is the biggest island of all.

New Guinea is an almost untouched island with few towns. Most of the native Papuan people live in rainforest villages.

New Caledonia is a tropical island with lush rainforests and coral reefs.

In **Australia**, cattle and sheep ranches are huge. The ranchers get to their herds on motorcycles and even by helicopter.

Sheep farming is important in **New Zealand**. Its beautiful mountains bring visitors from around the world, too.

The biggest rock in the world is deep in the Australian desert. It's called **Ayers Rock**.

The Opera House in **Sydney** has the shape of a sailing ship.

Children of Oceania

Peter lives in Melbourne, a big city in Australia. His mother drives him to school and gives him a packed lunch.

Yapa lives in Australia, too. He is an **Aborigine**, descended from the first inhabitants of this island. He plays an ancient musical instrument called a **didgeridoo**.

Sandy lives on a ranch deep in the Australian outback. She is far away from any school, so she hears her lessons by radio, and does her homework on her computer.

Greg lives in Auckland, New Zealand. He likes going to school, but he also likes playing **rugby**. Here, boys and girls both play the game.

Yumita is a Papuan girl. She and her village friends have a long walk through the rainforest to get to school.

Did You Know?

Peter, Yapa, Greg, and Sandy all speak English. They have an extra way of saying hello: G'day!

Hello!

Hi!

G'day!

Animals of Oceania

In Oceania, and especially in Australia, you can see animals that are not found anywhere else on Earth. Some of them are quite amazing!

Emus are huge birds that cannot fly. But they can run very fast on their big feet! The female emu lays the eggs, then the male sits on the nest until the chicks hatch.

Kangaroos are champion jumpers thanks to their strong hind legs and big back feet. They are **marsupials**: the female has a pouch on her belly. When a kangaroo **joey** is born it climbs into the pouch, where it drinks its mother's milk and grows. When it is big enough, the joey leaves the pouch.

The **echidna** has prickly spines, a long nose, and a sticky tongue to help it catch ants. The female lays her egg into a pouch on her belly — no need to make a nest for her baby!

Koala bears are marsupials. They live in the trees and eat eucalyptus leaves. Baby koalas ride piggyback on their mothers until they are ready to climb trees on their own.

The **cassowary** is a big bird that lives deep in the forest. It has a bony crest on its head, and it lays green-blue eggs.

Kiwis live only in New Zealand. Their feathers look like hairs, and their wings are so small that they cannot fly.

Figure It Out!

Who am I?

My snout looks like a duck's bill, and I have webbed feet.

I have brown fur, and a strong tail like a beaver's.

The females in my family lay eggs. The babies that hatch drink milk that seeps out of their mother's skin.

Answer: I am the duck-billed platypus, one of the most unusual animals in the world!

A Look at Europe

Europe is one of the smallest continents on Earth, but it is filled with lots of people.

The **fjords** of **Norway** are ancient mountain valleys that were flooded by the sea.

At **Stonehenge** in **England**, you can see a circle of tall standing stones that people put up thousands of years ago.

The **Eiffel Tower** is a famous metal tower in Paris, **France**. When it was built it was the highest structure in the world. Now it is the tallest building in Paris.

Vienna is the capital of **Austria**. Its opera house is one of the most famous in the world.

Prague, in the **Czech Republic**, is called the City of a Thousand Bells. That's because of its many churches.

The city of **Venice, Italy**, is built along water canals instead of main streets. People get around on water buses called **vaporettos**. Tourists sometimes travel the canals in little boats called **gondolas**.

Many houses on the islands of **Greece** are white, with blue windows and doors.

Number Time!

Europe is home to 48 different countries. It has over 100 cities. Nearly 720 million people live in Europe. Over 200 languages are spoken there.

Children of Europe

Timo lives in the far north of Europe, in Finland. In winter it is dark there many days because the sun does not rise. But in the summer the sun shines late into the night. It's called the midnight sun!

Gerda lives in Germany. Like all German kids, she goes to school in the morning, and can spend the afternoon playing sports, doing art, or making music.

Olena lives in Poland. Her house is made of wood, and is painted outside in bright colors. Her parents grow vegetables on their farm.

Maria lives in Spain. In summer when it is very hot, people stay indoors after lunch (it's called siesta time). They go out in the evening when the air is cooler.

Fergus lives in Scotland. In summer he goes to see amazing sports events. Men dressed in kilts throw heavy tree trunks as far as they can.

Eve lives in France. She can see the Eiffel Tower from her balcony in Paris. Eve and her family go to the beach for summer holidays.

Discovering the Poles

The North Pole and the South Pole are very cold places — so cold that the oceans nearby freeze over.

At the South Pole

The South Pole, or the **Antarctic**, is the coldest place on our planet. No people live there year-round. Only a few birds and marine mammals can withstand the temperatures.

Scientists come to the Antarctic to study its ice, weather, pollution, and animals. They arrive by boat in spring, live together on special **bases**, then leave at the end of summer.

Birth of a Baby Penguin

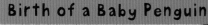

The **Emperor penguin** is a large sea bird.

The females lay a single egg, which the males keep warm in a fold on their bellies.

The males huddle together to protect themselves from the strong, icy winds.

When the penguin chick hatches, its mother hunts for fish to feed her baby.

At the North Pole

At the North Pole, or the **Arctic**, the frozen sea forms an ice-field or **glacier**. Not far from there live the Inuit of Canada and the U.S., and the Chukchi of Siberia.

Icebergs are huge blocks of ice that have broken off a glacier.

The Inuit still hunt seals, walruses, and narwhals (which have horns). They eat the meat and use the skins for clothing.

Today the Inuit live in modern houses painted all different colors.

Long ago when they lived by hunting, the Inuit built snow houses called **igloos**.

They sometimes still hunt using dog sleds, but mostly by snowmobile.

Life of the Chukchi

Anton lives in Siberia. His father raises a herd of reindeer.

Anton and his family live in a **uranga**, a tent made of wood posts and reindeer skins.

This is a big day. Anton will join in the reindeer festival.

They catch a young female reindeer with a rope **lasso**. Now they will make delicious cheese with her milk.

The Polar Bear

The polar bear is the largest of the bears. Its body helps it to live in the freezing cold of the Arctic.

Its small **ears** keep it from losing body heat.

Its **white fur** blends in with the snow, which helps it hunt. Underneath, its skin is black to soak up heat from the sun.

A thick **layer of fat** keeps the bear warm and helps it float in the water.

When a bear dives into the cold salt water, thin, transparent **eyelids** cover and protect its eyes, like diving goggles. It can close up its **nostrils**, too.

Its big **paws** act like snowshoes on the ice and snow. They have rough pads that keep the bear from slipping.

Number Time!

A polar bear can weigh as much as 500 kg (1,102 lb.), and standing up on its hind legs is taller than a tall man. A polar bear cub weighs less than 1 kg (2.2 lb.) at birth. Polar bears can live about 25 years.

Time to Eat

A polar bear moves along an ice floe, sniffing the air. He's not out for a walk — he's hunting for seals.

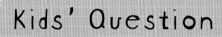

Kids' Question

Do polar bears attack people?

Normally polar bears avoid people, and are afraid of them. But they may attack if they think they are in danger. They are also quite curious, and will approach a town looking for food if they are hungry.

1

The bear hunts mostly with his sense of smell. He stands up on his hind legs to catch scent of his prey.

2

He approaches a hole in the ice as silently as possible. The moment a seal surfaces to breathe, the polar bear makes a grab for it.

Polar Bear Cousins

The **giant panda** is black and white. It lives in wooded areas of China and eats bamboo.

The **spectacled bear** of South America is named for the circles around its eyes.

3

The seal dives down and hides under the ice. The bear breaks the ice by dropping onto it with all his weight. Maybe he will catch the seal now?

4

But the seal is fast, and the polar bear often misses the mark. Luckily, this bear can go a long time between meals thanks to its fat reserves.

Brown bears live in North America, Asia, and Europe. The largest one is the **kodiak**, of North America.

Let's Protect Our Planet!

People are polluting the planet with their cars, their factories, and their waste. Today we realize that the climate is warming, animals are disappearing, and Earth is being damaged.

The Climate is Changing

It's warming up!

Over many years, scientists have studied how our planet's climate is getting warmer and warmer.

It's melting!

Bit by bit the warmer weather is melting ice at the Poles and on mountain tops.

It's scorching!

Deserts are getting bigger and bigger.

What's next?

Scientists think that the world's oceans are rising. Some islands may disappear, flooded by the higher ocean waters.

The Garbage Dumps Are Full

Candy wrappers, yogurt containers... What happens to all the things we throw in the garbage? Some waste goes to the dump where it is burned up. Glass, metal, paper, food scraps, and plastic can be recycled. That means they can be reused to make other things.

The Rainforests Are Shrinking

Every day, thousands of rainforest trees are cut down illegally. The exotic woods are used to make furniture. Trees are also chopped down to clear land for farming.

If we cut down the trees, the rainforest animals don't have a place to live, and certain species will disppear.

Dirty Oceans

When huge oil tankers spring leaks they spill oil out into the water. The thick, sticky petroleum covers the sea and washes onto the shore. Sea birds and marine mammals are harmed.

Kids' Question

What can I do to protect the planet?

- recycle
- buy things with less packaging
- take public transportation
- use less water
- turn off the lights when you don't need them
- put on a sweater instead of turning up the heat

The Universe

At night you can see thousands of the stars and planets that make up the universe. What you see is only a tiny part of what is out there!

The **Moon** circles the Earth. It is the Earth's satellite.

The **stars** are suns, like the Sun that lights and warms our planet Earth. These huge balls of burning gas give off a bright light. The stars don't disappear from the sky during the day. You just can't see them then because the light of the Sun is so strong.

You can see over **6,000 stars** with your naked eye. They look very small because they are so far away from Earth.

Long ago, people drew pictures of groups of stars so that they could remember where they were in the sky. These groups of stars are called constellations.

Try to find the Big Dipper constellation — it looks like a big spoon. Find it in the night sky where you live, too!

The Sun and the Earth belong to a **galaxy** made of billions of stars. It is called the **Milky Way**. Scientists say there are millions of galaxies in the universe.

The First Space Travelers

Bit by bit, by looking at the sky, building telescopes, making calculations, and traveling into space, we have learned more about our vast universe. But we still don't know the answers to all of our questions.

In the beginning, we sent animals rather than people into outer space. In 1958 the dog **Laika** was the first living creature to travel in space.

Russian astronaut **Yuri Gagarin** was the first person in space. In 1961 he circled Earth in a **space capsule**.

In 1965 **Valentina Tereshkova** became the **first female astronaut** to go up into space.

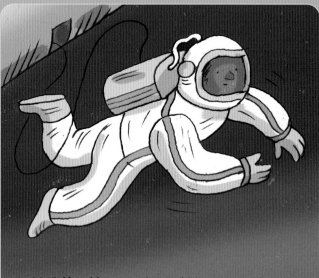

In 1965 **Alexei Leonov**, dressed in a space suit, was the first person to do a space walk.

How We Explore in Space

Powerful **rockets** shoot satellites, probes, and people into space. The rockets don't come back to Earth.

The **Space Shuttle** is how people get to space. It takes off on a big rocket, and lands back on Earth like a plane.

Space probes don't carry people. These machines explore distant planets, then send pictures and information back to scientists on Earth.

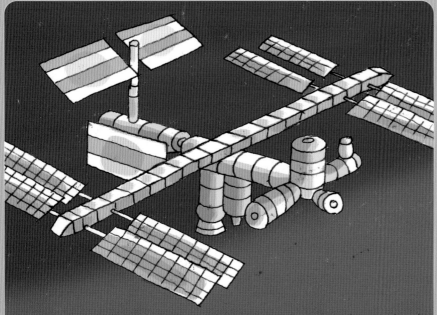

Astronauts and scientists from around the world stay on the **International Space Station** to do experiments and learn more about the universe.

Kids' Question

Are there extraterrestrials?

No one has ever seen an extra-terrestrial. Scientists are not sure if there is life on other planets as there is on Earth. The question is still open.

To the Moon!

In 1966 the Russian **space probe** *Luna 9* landed on the Moon to explore it.

In 1969, after a four-day voyage on the space capsule *Apollo 2*, American astronaut **Neil Armstrong** became the first man to walk on the Moon. He was joined by fellow astronaut **Ed Aldrin**. Together they planted an American flag on the lunar surface, and collected moon rocks to be studied after their return to Earth.

How We See into Outer Space

You can see some of the stars and the planets in our solar system by looking through a **telescope**.

Astronomers can see galaxies through giant telescopes in buildings called **observatories**.

Space telescopes circle the Earth and travel deep into space to send us pictures of the universe.

Radio telescopes listen for sounds from outer space.

The Earth and the Moon

The Moon circles the Earth. Both the Earth and the Moon circle around the Sun. But the Earth and the Moon are very different from each other.

On the Earth...

When you throw a ball in the air it always comes down to the ground. A force called gravity pulls it towards Earth. Without **gravity** you would float in the air!

Life is possible on Earth because our planet is covered in water and surrounded by a protective layer of air called the **atmosphere**.

Sunlight is made up of all the colors of the rainbow. But the atmosphere scatters so much blue light around that we see the sky as having a blue color.

The atmosphere contains oxygen, which allows us to breathe. Thanks to the atmosphere our planet is not too warm, and the Sun's fiery rays do not harm living things.

The atmosphere burns up most **meteorites**, pieces of space rock falling to Earth. We can see these as **shooting stars**.

Kids' Question

Why does the Moon change shape?

The Moon is round, but you don't always see all of it from Earth. The Moon moves across the sky and the part of the Moon that you see is the part that's lit up by the Sun. When the Sun lights up all of the Moon, you see a full moon in the sky. ◯ When only a bit of it is lit up, you see a crescent moon. ◗

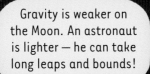

On the Moon...

Gravity is weaker on the Moon. An astronaut is lighter — he can take long leaps and bounds!

The temperatures are a lot less pleasant than on Earth: 100 °C (212 °F) during the day, and -150 °C (-238 °F) at night!

The sky is always dark, night and day.

There's no air on the Moon. Because air carries sound it is totally **silent** there.

People cannot breathe without oxygen. Luckily a **space suit** carries the oxygen an astronaut needs.

The Moon's surface is covered with **craters**, big holes dug by crashing meteorites.

The Solar System

The solar system has eight planets. They circle (orbit) around their star, the Sun. One of these is Earth, the planet we live on.

The **Sun** is an enormous ball of burning gases. Because it is bigger than the planets, its gravity pulls them to orbit around it. Huge explosions inside the Sun produce heat, and the light that shines on us.

These four are the smallest planets in the solar system. They are made of rock and have hard surfaces.

Mercury

Venus

Earth

Mars

Mercury is closest to the Sun. Like the Moon, its surface is covered with craters. It is very hot there by day: 400 °C (752 °F). **It orbits around the Sun over 88 days.**

Venus is surrounded by unbreathable gases. The hottest of the planets, it has a temperature of 470 °C (878 °F). **It orbits around the Sun over 225 days.**

Earth is your planet. It is the only planet in our solar system that can support life, so far as we know. **It orbits around the Sun over 365 days.**

Mars is called the Red Planet because of the color of its surface. It is very cold there. **It orbits around the Sun over 687 days.**

Did You Know?

These four planets are the biggest in the solar system. They are made of gas and don't have hard surfaces. They are all surrounded by rings made of dust and ice.

Neptune

Uranus

Saturn

Jupiter

Asteroids

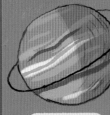

A band of rocks — or asteroids — orbits around the Sun between Mars and Jupiter.

Jupiter is the biggest planet in the solar system, with 16 moons that orbit around it. **It orbits around the Sun over 12 years.**

Saturn is circled by thousands of rings made of ice. **It orbits around the Sun over 30 years.**

Uranus is not visible to the naked eye. Pale green, it is surrounded by very thin rings. **It orbits around the Sun over 84 years.**

Like Uranus, Neptune is not visible to the naked eye. It is blue, and very strong winds blow there constantly. **It orbits around the Sun over 166 years.**

Comets

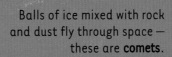

Balls of ice mixed with rock and dust fly through space — these are **comets**.

Living in Space

Jerry, Tim, and Sally are Canadian astronauts. These scientists are going to spend a few months in space.

1 In Training

In space, gravity is very low and everything floats. Before they leave, the astronauts learn to live without gravity by doing training exercises in water. They also prepare their bodies to withstand the force of lift-off.

2 Lift-Off

Jerry, Tim, and Sally are strapped into their seats on board the space shuttle that will take them to the International Space Station. It's time for lift-off! Two huge rockets propel the shuttle into space. Bye-bye, planet Earth!

Kids' Question

Can someone like me travel in space right now?

Kids can't travel in space now, but some non-scientists — very rich and very fit grownups — have. A few carefully chosen "space tourists" are allowed to spend time on the shuttle or the space station if they are willing to pay millions of dollars for the trip.

3 Station Life

Because everything floats on the space station, objects are attached to cables. The astronauts eat vacuum-packed foods and drink through straws. They move around by grabbing onto handles.

4 Exercise

Muscles get weaker in space. Jerry, Tim, and Sally need to do two hours of exercise every day to stay strong.

Did You Know?

Americans and Canadians call their space voyagers **astronauts**. The French call theirs **spationauts**, and the Russians call theirs **cosmonauts**.

5 Experiments

Jerry and Sally do experiments to learn how people, plants, and animals can best survive in space.

6 Repair Job

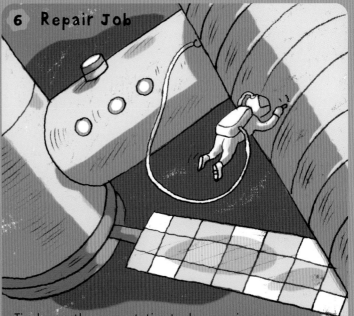

Tim leaves the space station to do a repair outside. He is attached by a cable to keep him from floating away. His space suit allows him to breathe, and keeps his body from getting too hot or cold.

Index